Praise for *13 Ways to Kill Your Community*

"13 Ways" has become my favorite handbook to help to motivate and educate community volunteer groups because it is 100% on the mark, highly readable, and funny to boot. Griffiths' depth of experience and analytical capacity allows him to get to the heart and gut of the factors that help and hinder community vitality."
    Liz Huff, Seeley's Bay (Leeds and 1000 Islands), Ontario

"I showed (13 Ways to Kill Your Community) to the village administrator and the next thing I knew, he wanted a dozen more for every department head. We handed out at least 30 books. There are lessons throughout the book for communities and the organizations within communities. For our community, the chapter on beautification had the greatest impact and resulted in real changes."
    Tim Evans, Rantoul, Illinois

"I've written several columns over the past couple years building off the themes in the book. Each chapter has good information easily applicable to our small town. This book is essential reading for anyone looking to improve the fortunes of their community."
    Reed Anfinson, Benson and Swift County, Minnesota

"Some communities thrive and grow while others die offer: for future generations. 13 Ways to Kill Your Community ¡ tools to choose either option for your community. If yoι one book on rural economic development, this is the onι most successful communities can improve and change for t
    John Ponikvar, Craig, Colorado

"After reading *13-Ways to Kill Your Community*, we had a dynamic conversation in our newsroom about how we could use it to editorialize on issues facing our rural communities. We started with the 'Don't Paint' chapter. Using information in the book, we told our readers they would find us setting the example, and encouraged others to follow. They did and our community is all the better for it."

Joey Young, Newton, Kansas

"This book looks deeply into why communities fail with examples from rural communities around North America. But then it goes on to explain how to turn that around to find success. This book presents an opportunity for us to look at our own towns, ask where we err, and then move on to success."

Becky Dickerson, St. John, Washington

"I loved the stories in the first edition. We read it for a book discussion hosted by the State Library of Iowa. We wanted to continue the conversation in our own communities, and to share the insights with council members, board members, staff, and anyone who cares about community. The book depicts the trials and tribulations of living and working in a small-town community so well. We hope to hear the live version at one of our conferences someday soon."

Roslin Thompson; Knoxville, Iowa

"If you're passionate about community building, this book is about to become your Bible! You'll find yourself nodding along as you picture your community while reading Doug's anecdotes. '13 Ways' has been very influential to us — a group of young people trying to create positive change in our small community. Doug has been an incredible resource via both the book and his knowledgeable consulting; I highly recommend both!"

Dr. Amanda Hill, Pulse Pictou County, New Glasgow, Nova Scotia

13 Ways to
Kill Your Community

Written By Doug Griffiths, MBA

With Kelly Clemmer

ISBN
978-1-4602-9757-5 (Hardcover)
978-1-4602-9758-2 (Paperback)
978-1-4602-9759-9 (eBook)

Cover Artwork: Mr Rick Sealock
Author Photo: Mr. Rocco Macri (www.macriphotography.com)
Foreword by Mr Paul McNeill

Published by 13 Ways Inc
3400 Manulife Place
10180 – 101 Street
Edmonton, AB T5J 3S4
(587) 573-1313 | 13ways.ca
info@13ways.ca

Library and Archives Canada Cataloguing in Publication

Griffiths, Doug, author
    13 ways to kill your community / written by Doug Griffiths,
    with Kelly Clemmer. -- Second edition.

    Issued in print and electronic formats.
    ISBN 978-1-4602-9758-2 (paperback).--ISBN 978-1-4602-9757-5
    (hardback).--ISBN 978-1-4602-9759-9 (ebook)

    1. Community development--Canada. 2. Rural development--Canada. 3. Community leadership--Canada. I. Clemmer, Kelly, author II. Title. III. Title: Thirteen ways to kill your community.

HN110.Z9C6 2016   307.1'40971   C2016-905840-9
                                     C2016-905841-7

 FriesenPress

Suite 300 - 990 Fort St
Victoria, BC, V8V 3K2
Canada

www.friesenpress.com

1. BUSINESS & ECONOMICS, COMMERCE

Distributed to the trade by The Ingram Book Company

Dedication

I dedicate this book to all those community builders who work to make their community stronger. I know why you do it. It is why I do it too. We will find a way.

Acknowledgements

My family, especially my wife, who knows how passionate I am about this. You give tirelessly to me, so that I can give tirelessly to communities. You endure long weeks while I am away, lonely nights as I sit and write, and still smile at me when I finally get back home.

David and Rose Scollard who took a chance on me to make the first edition of this book possible. They say they are my biggest fans. The feeling is mutual. Our work together exceeded our wildest dreams.

Kelly Clemmer who encouraged me to make my presentation into a book, followed up by putting all my presentations together on paper, and then helped make sense of them.

All those who shared, and continue to share, your stories, your experiences, your pains, and your successes.

This book is for all of you.

TABLE OF CONTENTS

FOREWORD

I remember the moment I knew Doug Griffiths was the real deal. He had already mesmerized the delegation attending the Georgetown Conference with his smart, insightful and sassy, *13 Ways to Kill Your Community* presentation. During the question and answer session that followed a Mi'kmaq delegate asked for advice on a particularly difficult situation she faced in her community. Perhaps realizing the question required a more thoughtful discussion than would occur in front of 250 delegates, Doug said he would be happy to talk to her after the session.

Some speakers would leave it at that, knowing that the discussion could easily be avoided. Not Doug Griffiths. He sought the lady out and they found a quiet spot in King's Playhouse to strategize about the best path forward. He listened. They talked it through. He wanted to help her find a solution. He wanted to help them find the way to success. I remember how impressed I was knowing that Doug was going far beyond the typical role of conference speaker. He cared. He still does, and it shows.

Atlantic Canada faces many issues. Our population is dramatically aging (average age in my hometown of Montague, PEI is 47), our youth believe their future lies in larger centres, our traditional industries of fishing and farming and tourism often feel the squeeze of economic ups and downs, and we struggle to tear down silos that stop us from effectively dealing with the big issues we face. We realized we had to do something. The first Georgetown Conference in 2013 was a grassroots effort to empower 'doers and producers' in our Atlantic Canadian communities to find solutions that would work at the local level. It was not going to be a typical conference.

We did not ask government for one cent in funding. We didn't want it to be a government event. In fact, no provincial or federal politicians were allowed. It's not that we felt politicians could not contribute. We simply realized we didn't need anyone looking for photo ops or dolling out promises. We wanted our folks to find their own solutions, and to own their community's future. As Doug would say, it wasn't an event for the people of power, it was an event for the homegrown people of influence. As such, every delegate was required to complete an application to attend and if you happened to be a consultant or bureaucrat with a government funded organization your chances of winning admittance were greatly reduced.

Our no politician rule caused us more than a little consternation when we became aware of *13 Ways to Kill Your Community* and Doug Griffiths. The book is a must read for anyone struggling to overcome entrenched beliefs and political realities that too often stagnate growth and opportunity. But how would we get around the rule of no politicians, especially one from the other side of the country. We took the risk and discovered that in person, Doug is not a politician. He is just a man committed to help us get rid of the chains we place around ourselves, chains that hold us back, and to help us get on with building stronger communities.

The brilliance of 13 Ways is the cutting simplicity with which it is written and the style in which it is presented. The stories he tells are seen in every town. Atlantic Canada is not unique. Communities across North America face growing challenges that need to be addressed. It doesn't matter if you live in Alberta or Prince Edward Island, Iowa or Illinois, Ontario or Colorado, all of our communities face challenges. The solutions he presents to overcome those challenges are simple, basic and effective. They are implementable anywhere, and can get you started down the path to success.

When we decided to host Georgetown 2.0 in June 2016 we employed a format that was very much delegate driven. Rather than the traditional conference of people talking from a stage down to an audience, we relied on delegates driving creation of the agenda. There were only two keynote speakers, Chef Michael Smith of Food Network Canada fame who has built a burgeoning global media empire from the tiny hamlet of Fortune, Prince Edward Island, and once again Doug Griffiths. We needed strong speakers who would push delegates beyond their comfort zone. Both of our speakers delivered in spades.

Change in small towns is difficult. Often change has to come slowly and incrementally. Some days you may not even be sure you are making progress as you take three or four steps back in the hope of making one small step forward. It can be difficult to deal with, and often becomes discouraging if not completely disheartening. Doug demonstrates through this book we are not alone. He shows us the issues we face are similar and universal. He also helps jar people out of their slumber so you can make strides instead of incremental change, so you can step through issues instead of around them.

In my region seven small communities are navigating the thorny path of trying to negotiate shared services and potentially a regional form of government. In many places it is hard to get a community to work together. It is even more difficult to get neighbouring communities to work together so they can have the capacity to grow, instead of simply holding on for dear life. Doug helped pave the road for these discussions. He helps ensure the discussions that need to be had are had by the community.

I wish everyone could read this book before they get into trouble, but no matter the challenge, no matter the bump in the road that just dislodged you, or the wall that stands in your way there is never a bad time to be inspired. There is never a bad time to read this book. His book is legendary in my tiny province as it still gets passed from person to person and community to community. People still talk about his presentations across the region. He continues to inspire people long after he has returned home and that means he has had a major impact on our Maritime communities.

I am sure this book will have a lasting impact on you and your community too. It is the type of leadership, and strong helping hand, at a time when our communities and those that care about them, desperately need it.

Paul MacNeill
Founder — The Georgetown Conference

PROLOGUE

Welcome to the second edition of what has become colloquially known simply as *13 Ways*. In the time that has passed since the first edition, a great deal has changed. I have presented "13 Ways" to conferences and communities across the country, and across the continent. I have also provided strategic advice to communities, organizations and leaders in both the private and public sectors about the strategies they need for success, although sometimes the advice is still as simple as how they can stop sabotaging their own futures. It seems the concept of *13 Ways* and the insights it is meant to provide have expanded beyond application just in communities. Those not focused primarily on the future of their town have also found meaning in the concepts and insights in these pages, which are now being used by folks in their businesses, in their organizations and in their personal lives as well.

The biggest change for me since the first edition was published in 2010 came with my resignation from politics in January 2015, after 13 years of public service. When first elected I was the youngest sitting politician in the Legislature and the sixth youngest to be elected in almost 100 years. In my four elected terms I served as senior Cabinet Minister of two portfolios, including Municipal Affairs; in three junior cabinet portfolios, including Finance and Agriculture; and as a member of Treasury Board for the Government Legislature for four years. When I resigned I was one of the more experienced politicians still in office, but I was also still one of the youngest in the Legislature. The experiences I had were both broad and deep. They changed me as a person, increased my wisdom and gave me valuable tools to assist people and communities in my life after politics. In every capacity in which I served I focused my attention and maintained my commitment to building prosperous communities. I resigned so I could return to working on helping people, businesses, organizations and communities through "13 Ways."

Before I ever became an elected official, I was a rancher and a teacher. I loved to teach, but it was also a good job to have in a rural community and it provided the income I needed to subsidize my ranching addiction. I have a teaching degree, but that was preceded by an Honors Degree in Philosophy with an unofficial double minor in both Political Science and Eastern Religion. Yes, Eastern Religion — Taoism, Buddhism, Confucianism, Jainism and so on. Not very practical when it comes to feeding the cows, but valuable when you are young and seeking both answers about, and a purpose for, your life. Both degrees are from the University of Alberta and at the time of this writing have I completed the Executive MBA program, also at the University of Alberta. I do like my education.

Originally, however, going to university was less about learning and more about getting out of town. I, like so many other young people from small towns, had big plans to do some big things with big people in the big city. I finished my philosophy studies with the full intent of pursuing a law degree and getting a job at some prestigious firm that would handle important cases, and I was going to be right there in the thick of it. However, when I finished my first degree, I realized I wanted to do big things, but I didn't really want to do them with big people in the big city . . . and I realized I didn't want to be a lawyer. It is not that I don't like the city or city people at all. I lived in the city for many years. I simply realized I wanted to ranch and I wanted to teach, and I wanted to do these things in a smaller place where I had space for my mind, body and soul to breathe and to wander. After the philosophy degree and some time on my horse and feeding my cows, I decided to get a teaching degree. It meant I could continue to work and live in my community. It meant I could make enough money to support my ranching habit, and it meant I could be home.

I was happy. I had grown up on the family farm and I could still work on it. I could still have some cows, and I could still ride my horse. I was teaching in a very small school where the students and staff were exceptional and I was enjoying personal success. When I wasn't working on our farm or teaching, I was taking the students skating, or helping with some work on their family farms and occasionally dabbling in politics. I had everything I ever wanted.

I recall, however, sitting in the White Goose Restaurant across the street from a house I was considering buying. I was looking for a house well suited and well located for present and future needs and I was sure it was there, right across the street in that beautiful little town of Castor. Thirty minutes to the south was the school where I would be teaching, and twenty minutes to the east was the farm where I would work after school. As I finished off my second cup of coffee it struck me that I wasn't thinking about whether this house or its yard would be big enough for when I married and had children, or even if the house had a good foundation or a nice view. Instead, I wondered if the town I wanted to live in, situated between the town where I taught and the town where I farmed, all three of which I loved so, would still be there as the years went on. I found myself sitting in that coffee shop regularly with the other coffee shop regulars lamenting the situation of our community and all other rural communities. I often wondered aloud, "When will someone do something to make it better?"

Then I realized, I was somebody. I realized if I was going to enjoy the life I wanted, if I was going to continue to teach in that small community, to farm in the other and live in the one that lay between the two, it was going to be my responsibility to find a way to make our rural communities stronger, better and as enduring as time. Eventually I found the woman of my dreams and we had two sons, and the depth of my sense of responsibility and passion grew from being personal to being generational. I wanted, and still want, my sons to be able to grow up in a good community of their choosing; big or small.

So, I became more and more involved in politics, speaking and listening to anyone willing to discuss the issue of rural and community development. I wrote columns in newspapers, I wrote letters and I gave advice to anyone in a position of power who would listen. Then the chance to be our local representative in the Legislature came up and I could not resist running in the by-election to fill the vacancy. Despite a few snickers about my age and some comments that I didn't stand a chance, I ran and I won. Make no mistake, the irony of giving up my full-time rural life, riding my horse and teaching my students, for a life that took me to the city, away from my horses and cows and students for extensive periods of time, was not lost on me. I did it so our communities could have a chance for enduring prosperity and success and to help those communities that have the same goal.

I campaigned in that nomination and the by-election on the need to promote rural development and the need to build stronger communities. In fact, I campaigned through each and every election on that very platform, and included that as a central plank in my failed bid to become party leader in 2011. I dedicated each and every term to working on building stronger communities. I am proud of the work we accomplished over the years, and I wouldn't change a thing. I had the pleasure of co-authoring a report that listed over 72 recommendations about how to strengthen our communities. The report covered health care, education, community infrastructure, economic development, youth, seniors, Aboriginals, immigrants, arts and culture, the environment, water, transportation, infrastructure, trade and tourism. In my first three years I travelled to over 200 communities, but by the end of my political career I'd had the pleasure of visiting closer to 400. It was an amazing experience. For a man who likes his education I have to say the experiences I gleaned over that time gave me the best education on community building I could have hoped for.

The report was well received and I was invited all over to speak about its recommendations, so I went through all of them with every community I visited. I also heavily emphasized two other points I had learned. First, if our communities were going to prosper over the long-term, it was essential that every level of government realized the role it would need to play in laying down the foundations for success. Whether local/municipal, state/provincial, or federal, each level must be constantly vigilant in pursuing its role in community development. This includes such steps as creating a strong underlying infrastructure, minimizing encumbrances to growth through reduced regulations and paperwork, and developing support systems for the exchange of information about best practices.

Unquestionably the various levels of government play an important role in this process, but it is of the greatest importance to realize they do not have the ultimate responsibility. That responsibility rests with those in the community. That is why the second and most important point I always made was that the only way to ever ensure the long-term success of any community is for the community itself to decide it wants to be successful.

I know it sounds trite and banal, but I suggest to you that even the most contentious and complex of challenges often has a very simple solution we may have overlooked. Perhaps it is because, as intelligent beings, we believe truth must lie in complexity, or perhaps we are just too ashamed that we often cannot recognize the simplest of solutions. I believe that ultimately it is simply easier to assign responsibility to someone else so we can carry on with our own personal stresses. Regardless of the situation, a community's future truly rests within its own populace and their desire to achieve success. It is just that simple. In fact, I suggest a community that believes it will succeed cannot be stopped by government or money. Conversely, a community that believes it will fail cannot be saved by government or money.

I am sure a government agency could ride into town on a white horse with a generic plan and some money to execute it, and might achieve some short-term success. However, if the community members themselves don't write their own plan for success then they won't truly believe in it as a community, and there won't be the commitment to follow through with the plan over the long-term. This exact scenario happens over and over with government programs of this nature, and invariably the plans fall to the wayside and collect dust when the money is gone. In the end, nothing long-term has been accomplished and no permanence is achieved, save for a few people who can now feel better about themselves for trying, and a few others who can now blame failure on the withdrawal of the government entity and its money.

I emphasized in the report and with every speech I gave that without the community's buy-in, without their own members' determination, virtually any rural development project would be doomed to failure. If the community simply waited for me or anyone else in government to make all its worries and problems go away, then we were all wasting energy, because every community is different and every community has different issues and I can't know them all, or turn all the wrongs into rights. A government solution would be an ineffective, generic solution. If their notion was the money that followed was the answer and everything would be just fine with continued funding, then we were just wasting taxpayers' money as well. Money is not usually the answer to a problem, because the lack of money is not what the real problem is. I know this will be a controversial claim, but my experience is that adding money to a problem right up front doesn't fix the problem, it only buys us a little time. Money up front causes us to lose focus; to lose our resolve, and that means we will end up right back where we started because we never went after the root of the problem. It is true that when a real solution is finally found and implemented it may take a little money, but if the solution starts with money, it will fail because it will only be a mask, not a solution that comes from the community.

Communities have to assess their own strengths and weaknesses, and analyze what are the greatest risks and what new opportunities are awaiting them. Communities have to make a conscious choice if they want to be successful or not, and not lay responsibility on someone else or simply on the need for money. Communities have to determine what it is they can and must do to be successful. Communities have to believe they *can be* successful, and their plan *will* make them successful, and they must then follow through on *their* plan with enduring commitment. In fact, enduring commitment really is the only way to get enduring success. Communities have to believe they can achieve their goals with or without government participation, and with or without government money. If they don't do so, any slight success will only last until the government or money runs out on them . . . and it always will. If they accept they must do it themselves and have a real commitment to seeing their community succeed, nothing can stop them.

I passed this on at each presentation I made, but I wasn't sure if those listening really got the message. Once, I was on my way to one particular community for the third time to give my rural community development speech. The first two times I had done the presentation I got the same reaction. They loved what I said. They listened to the message I emphasized so passionately about *their* role in making *their* community strong. A few weeks after each presentation, however, they called me up and asked how long it would be until they saw some commitment (read: money) from the government on the report. They had missed the core of the message. They wanted the government to fix "it," and they wanted government money to backstop "it." But they didn't seem to know or care what "it" was, and they missed the point that "it" was all in their hands, if they really wanted to fix "it." They wanted the government to do it for them. Frankly, they wanted anyone else to do it for them. They wanted to leave it in the hands of someone else to decide what was wrong with the community and what the solution should be, and then to fund it. But governments don't actually do that work very well. They may try really hard, but in honesty they are simply policy and funding agencies and don't do well at truly fixing "its," especially those community level "its."

Governments make rules to protect people who make stupid choices, but inevitably some people make even stupider choices no one could have imagined. They make rules to stop people from ever hurting themselves, but eventually people will find new ways to hurt themselves despite those rules. Governments make laws designed to protect people from losing their fortunes to con artists, yet people somehow find new ways to give their money away to obvious fraudsters. The government cannot fix people's problems like we hope it can. Yet, we look to government like it is a fresh god, arrived to grant our wishes and protect us from our enemies, and the hallowed halls of its buildings are the new place to light candles and lay down prayers. Honestly, I doubt the government can fix *any* person's problem if the person involved doesn't want to fix it themselves — and if they want to fix it themselves, they very rarely need the government's help in the first place. It's all about people, the choices they make and the attitudes they have, as it always has been. The people of any community are the catalysts for its success or failure. They own it, whether they want to or not.

So, as I drove to that particular community for the third time to speak about my report and its recommendations, my frustration grew at the thought of them calling me again to ask when I would fix their mess; the one they had the power to fix themselves. I started to think about all of the communities I had been to and all the ones I'd witnessed making choices that were sabotaging their own success. That's when the epiphany struck me.

When I was a teacher, on occasion I spoke to high school students about what factors were important to become successful in life; such as study hard, work hard, don't do drugs and marry someone nice. Those are all important elements to achieve success in life. The students and I had good discussions. One day I realized, however, those conversations didn't inspire a single one of them to do one single thing different with their lives or the choices they were making. As they walked out of the room the words and ideas we spoke of remained at their desks, as if they were old class notes to be cleaned up and disposed of by the janitor at the end of the day. They understood what I said. They really did get it. Parents and teachers had been saying those very words to them for years. The elements of a good life weren't a surprise to them or anyone else, but what we had discussed was entirely about the future. The future didn't really connect with what they were doing today. It didn't actually lead the students to consider today's decisions, or consider the impact their potentially poor behavior today could have on their futures. I could tell my well-intended words were simply not going to make them change.

I decided, therefore, the change would have to start with *me*, by means of a totally different approach. The next time I walked into a classroom to hold the discussion with the students I started by asking them to paint a picture of what their life would be like in the future if they considered it to be a failure. Yes, you read that right, but I'll repeat it anyway. I asked students to describe to me what their futures would look like if they considered their lives a failure. It took a little time and patience, but after a bit of encouragement and explanation they understood what I was seeking and we were on a roll.

They started describing a failed life to me and to each other. I got descriptions like, "I'd be a drug addict," "I'd get pregnant or get someone pregnant before I was ready to take on the responsibilities of raising a family," and "I would fail out of school, so I couldn't get a good job."

Once we had a good list and a good discussion the next question came. I asked them to pretend any one of the scenarios we had discussed was their actual goal; what they wanted to achieve . . . and then I asked them to consider what they needed to do today to get there. "For instance," I said, "if your goal is to become a drug addict, because you want to fail in life and you want to do it that way, how would you start toward that goal today?"

After a pause, someone put up their hand and said, "Well, if I wanted to become a drug addict and start right away, I would start by smoking a joint this weekend." A couple of students turned red with embarrassment, because that was what they had done the last weekend. Those students had thought smoking a joint was harmless, and perhaps it was. Certainly the majority of folks who smoke a joint don't turn into hard-core drug addicts, but hard-core drugs addicts don't get their start by snorting cocaine or injecting heroin at their first soiree either. They start small and with something seemingly innocent.

We went through the items on the list one by one, and figured out for each one what we could do today to be sure to achieve the goal of failing at life. When we got to the premature pregnancy question, I asked how they could start right now to get to that goal. The students blushed over the impure thoughts they were having, and then we all laughed. Eventually they recognized they would have to have unprotected sex in order to achieve the goal of getting pregnant now. Some of the students suddenly looked nervous, because they had been doing exactly that. When we started to talk about failing out of school, which would mean they couldn't get a good job and take care of their families, they suggested the best way to start would be to fail a test they had coming up in any one of their classes.

At that point they all started to look a little nervous as though they had a sudden inclination to study more, immediately. They all began to look at how the actions they were making today could have long-term ramifications on their lives, though none of them wanted those ramifications or to fail in life. The impact was unmistakable.

We all have goals and dreams. We all have visions and plans for what our future will entail, and sometimes we even have a roughly drawn roadmap on how to get there. Almost daily, however, we do things that sabotage those goals and dreams. The connection between what we do today and what we're striving for tomorrow is often not made because it is hard to be eternally conscious of how every single choice we make fits in with our long-term plans or where it fits on our roughly hewn roadmap. So, many of those particular daily decisions and choices are exactly those we would make if our goal was to ruin our lives, though that isn't really our goal. The challenge is that we often forget our long-term plans in our immediate choices and we unthinkingly trade away what we want most for what we want now. Hormone-laced high school students are a prime example of this, but they are far from exclusive future members of the broken dreams club.

Those kids who smoked a joint over the weekend weren't trying to become drug addicts. The students having unprotected sex weren't trying to get pregnant or get some deadly STD. The students who weren't studying weren't trying to fail out of school so they would get poor jobs. Yet, in each of those cases, if the goal was to ruin their life, each of those students who made such a poor choice had taken the exact first step they needed in order to achieve that goal to perfection. Many of the students walked away from those discussions and came back later to tell me they completely changed their lives because of it. Many parents came back to thank me because it had changed their high school students' lives when it seemed nothing else would. A few parents even came back to tell me it had caused them to change their own daily choices so they could change the course their lives were on. As I said before, full-grown adults are just as likely to make day-to-day decisions equally destructive to the goals and dreams they so eagerly seek as any teenager.

I came to the realization what worked to help turn young people's lives around could also work to help turn communities around. Communities all want to be successful and they all have hopes and dreams and plans . . . and oh my they have a lot of plans . . . for their future. Yet, every single one of them makes decisions that may feel right, may seem minor and inconsequential, or may simply suit their short-term needs, but nevertheless are decisions that sabotage their long-term goals, and their chance for long-term success. They don't connect how the actions and decisions they make today undermine the vision they have for their community tomorrow. It occurred to me perhaps the same exercise that had changed the students' lives for the better could be performed with the communities that were unwittingly sabotaging their futures.

So, on my way back to the community to speak for the third time, I carefully began to write down some of the ways I had seen communities ruining their own futures with the decisions they were making, or not making, every single day. I actually came up with 10 ways I had witnessed communities sabotage their own success and did a 15-minute presentation on them. As time went on I did the presentation more, and I fleshed it out a bit with some examples. The more I spoke, the more stories communities shared on what they had done to fail, and so the more stories I had to share. The number of ways just kept growing. Some merged with others. Stories continued to be told and shared, and the presentation continued to evolve. Eventually I settled on 13 themes, and the number seemed particularly fitting for the topic since "13" is considered unlucky, and "Killing Your Community" seems equally undesirable. I recognize the list is not exhaustive, and indeed, I am making notes and collecting new stories for a potential *13 MORE Ways to Kill Your Community.* You can very likely think of dozens more ways communities destroy their own futures, and you are welcome to share if you like.

The point to this book and to the presentation I give to accompany it, is not to be a list of things you actually want to do. The point is our hopes and dreams are often shattered by actions we do daily that may be causing negative consequences for the future of our communities. It is my hope this book will help you recognize those activities and actions, but that would still only be a treatment of the symptoms, not the real cause of failure. Ultimately, it is my objective to help you recognize the cause of failure is rooted entirely in the attitudes that are behind those actions. Our attitudes ultimately drive the way we see the world, they drive the way we respond to it, and they drive the choices we make. It is our attitudes that ultimately lead to our success or our failure as communities, organizations, businesses, industries and ultimately . . . as the human race.

There is something from the previous paragraph that bears repeating because of its significance. Every single one of the 13 Ways outlined within this book is about the attitudes we have, because ultimately they are what cause our success, or our own destruction. The students' choice to do drugs, or have unprotected sex, or fail school is not nearly as important as the students' recognition of the attitudes that led to those choices, because recognition of the impact of wrong attitudes is what drives permanent change. Making different choices can be hard for any of us. We want what we want. However, when we recognize how the wrong attitude leads to our own destruction we can't help but change our attitudes, and when we change our attitudes our choices change all by themselves to suit the new attitude. That is what helped the students (as well as some parents) to change. Creating the right attitude takes a lot of work, but the first step is to recognize when an attitude is self-destructive and negative. That can be a painful realization and therefore not one made easily. But once that happens, once you see it, you can't un-see it. Once you recognize it, it actually takes will power to not change. It is the same for communities, or organizations, or businesses. Sabotaging your community's success; killing your community, all comes down to attitude. Change the attitude and you can change the fate of your community. That is what this book is about.

I don't name any particular community in this book because 13 years in politics has taught me naming names is not always helpful and can serve as a distraction. It doesn't matter which community was self-destructing. What matters is recognizing the attitude that caused it, and to identify ways to remedy it. I have also realized there is more value in the story than there is in the name. After reading the first edition of the book, a young woman in Texas who had asked me to come to speak also asked me to confirm that one of the stories was about her hometown. I politely said, "No." She said she understood why I didn't want to name any town but begged me to confirm that I had written about that small Texas town, because what I had written was uncannily accurate to the events that transpired there. It couldn't be a coincidence, she insisted. I continued to assert the story was not about her town. She still didn't believe me, and at one point laughed and suggested I might be lying. I finally convinced her I had never heard of her town, and in fact, I had not yet ever been to Texas. She couldn't believe another town halfway across the continent could have done the exact same thing as her own hometown. It confirmed the value of these stories is not in seeing the names but in seeing the attitudes, because these are attitudes that exist in virtually every single community. We see ourselves in the stories, we recognize the attitudes that cause failure, and when we do that, we change.

This book is written in the first person because it is based on the "13 Ways to Kill Your Community" speech I have been giving for a few years, but my friend Kelly Clemmer was instrumental in helping the book come into existence. When I decided to run in that very first election it was at Kelly's office I made one of my first stops, and it was at his encouragement I wrote the first series of "13 Ways" into a set of weekly newspaper columns. Kelly was with the Wainwright newspapers from 1999 until 2015, and at our first meeting in 2002 had been an editor for about a year. He has moved onto new adventures now, but he continues to serve his local community at every turn.

Kelly helped *Star News* earn a number of awards, including Best Overall Newspaper within its circulation class, and two Golden Dozen editorial writing awards from the International Society of Weekly Newspaper Editors (ISWNE) The first edition of this book was made possible because of Kelly's hard work at turning my words into prose when I was far too busy to write.

Kelly was also involved in this project because he is one of the most community-minded people I have ever met. He chaired the Centennial Celebration Committees for both the Province of Alberta's Centennial in 2005 and the Town of Wainwright's Centennial in 2008. He is a founding member of the Wainwright Arts Festival and the founding chair of the Wainwright Arts Council, and from 2004 to 2007 was a member-at-large for the Writers Guild of Alberta. He sat on the Wainwright Habitat for Humanity board, and also served on the executive International Society of Weekly Newspaper Editors board from 2009 to 2015 and as president in 2013-2014. He was awarded the 2009 Citizen of the Year award by the Wainwright and District Chamber of Commerce for his volunteering and organizing efforts in the community. As these awards attest, he has done incredible work in helping to bring arts to his community and in helping its members enhance their quality of life.

Welcome to *13 Ways to Kill Your Community*.

CHAPTER 1
FORGET THE WATER

The evolution of humanity can be seen in the development of its communities. I'll speak more of this in a later chapter, but essentially communities formed out of a need for security and protection. As the risk and threat of immediate harm lessened, early community-dwellers were able to turn their focus and their daily aspirations to initiatives that would improve their well being. Growing more food and learning new skills led to a barter and exchange system that created economic trade. That development improved efficiencies and the use of resources in a way that increased overall wealth for individuals, families and communities, and led — and still leads today — to a progressively better quality of life where basic needs, and much more than our basic needs, are met. That is the story, greatly oversimplified, of why communities formed and how they led to increased prosperity.

This explanation, however, misses one critical element that would have had to be in place for any of that history to occur. All communities throughout human history have formed, evolved and grown because they were located at, or near, a river, lake, or ground aquifer that could supply the residents with water. Water is the foundational resource on which communities build. As my grandpa so eloquently put it to me when I was young; "You can go three minutes without air, three days without water, and three weeks without food. You can do without just about everything else you can imagine." Without water, you die. We have seen many communities throughout history suffer and die when they didn't have enough water. Sometimes the quality of the water was an issue; the result of contamination, and other times it was simply an absence of water altogether. Regardless, a lack of quality, or the lack of quantity of water is enough to kill your community.

We can all recall recent examples of communities that have experienced water quality issues that were catastrophic, such as Walkerton in Canada, and Flint in the United States. On many occasions community members were made violently ill by an "event" that caused the water to become contaminated. Some of the more horrific events lead to tragic deaths and made national and international headlines. Such an event is horrible for people and for communities to experience, but those events have also led to improvements and new investments in basic community water infrastructure in recent years. Yet we are far from ensuring the problem never happens again. Every month across Canada and the United States there are multiple communities issued boil-water orders because of health risks associated with the quality of water. Those boil-water orders aren't what concern me, however. Those orders mean we are catching the challenges before they cause negative consequences. The one that worries me is the one that isn't caught in time. Just because we are better at making sure we don't experience acute impacts on our water quality doesn't mean our work and the investments that are necessary are done. Acute contamination of water can kill a community, but it can also kill residents. The security of the quality of our water is not something we can afford to take for granted.

Those acute contamination issues seem to be the real headline grabbers and the issues we usually focus on, but water quality is about much more than just guaranteeing our water doesn't kill us or make us violently ill when we drink it. I have stayed in a lot of communities over the many years I have been working with them, and I have found a correlation between the quality of the water in the community and the state of the community overall. Blindfold me, take me into virtually any community in North America and sit me down at a kitchen table in one of the homes with a glass of water from the kitchen tap. When you remove the blindfold I can tell you the state of the community based on the quality of water in the glass. If the water is discolored, has a strange or bad smell, has a bad taste, has a lot of gas in it, or shows poor quality in any other way, the community will almost certainly have serious shortcomings of its own. That community with the poor quality of water will almost always have grungy, dirty streets, boarded-up windows on empty businesses, old unkempt houses, and no new subdivisions. Essentially the town will look like it is dying.

If that glass of water is clean and clear, on the other hand, if it doesn't have a bad smell and it has a "quality taste" to it — I know, that's hard to define, but you know what I mean — then I will see a different town. There is a good chance when I walk out the door of the house I'll see new businesses, clean streets and washed windows, new homes, plenty of flowers planted and in general a town that looks alive. Of course, there is no assurance a town with quality water will be a raging success. There are many towns I have helped over the years that have quality water but still struggle to find ways to achieve enduring prosperity. The point is communities that *don't* have quality water are *always* failing, and won't be successful. Through my experiences, it has become painfully obvious to me communities that don't have quality water need not expend effort on any other initiatives because nothing will improve until the quality of the water improves. The reason is very simple. People demand good-quality water.

Actually, that isn't true either. People do not demand quality water anymore. They used to, but now people don't demand it, they simply expect it. People won't tolerate anything less than quality water, and you can check this out for yourself. Spend some time in your local gas station. Buy a cup of coffee and sit by the front counter for a half hour and listen to people who come through. You will probably hear every person who comes into the station complain about the price of gas, but they will not say a word about the price of the bottle of water they are purchasing. By volume those bottles used to be three times the price of gasoline. Now, water can be bought in bulk cases for cheap, but in individual bottles it is still often twice the price as the gasoline we buy, and the water is really nothing more than decent tap water. People simply expect good-quality water. They don't demand it out loud anymore. They simply won't settle for less.

The quality of water we expect has gone far beyond only what we drink, however. Very few people in North America are willing to buy a house with water stains running down the tub or around the drain in the sink. Sure, some might tolerate this sort of blemish in a very old building, but they would probably figure the stains were old and wouldn't return once the sink and tub were replaced. Very few, if any, people purchasing a relatively new house would accept staining, given all the implications, real or imagined, that come with it. With stained fixtures come questions about the quality of water, and potential health worries of drinking it, showering in it and washing clothes in it. The natural inclination on the purchaser's part would be to wonder about the longevity of the fixtures and appliances and, even more worrisome, to wonder about the soundness of the internal structural components of the house, such as the hot water heater and the plumbing. The water may cause only the stains and nothing more, but the majority of people aren't interested in finding out. They won't tolerate the problem, which means they won't buy the house — and they might just decide not to live in the community at all.

In one particular community a discussion about the town's water issues raged for over 15 years. Almost an entire generation's worth of time had been spent complaining about the issues and fighting about the solutions. The town had a reputation for its poor-quality water. It definitely left stains around the drains. I visited one young couple in that community who had moved into a brand-new house in a brand-new subdivision. The house was so new the front steps were still a temporary wood frame, but there in their brand-new, white bathroom sink and tub were the beginnings of yellow stains. It turned them off and they joined the fight to improve the town's water quality. The discoloration was not a real health issue — it was more an issue about the perception of quality. There *was* a health-issue concern about the water in the community, though, because the sodium content was very high. The level was well within all the health and water-quality guidelines, but everyone still felt uneasy about it. The town became famous for all the wrong reasons, as I realized myself when I heard the community described as the place to go if you want to develop a heart condition. Not a very nice reputation to have, indeed. Yet, for 15 years neither the perception nor the reality of the quality of the water in that community was addressed.

Some communities have substantive and chronic water-quality issues, while others have difficulties that are more cosmetic. Whatever the nature of the problem, if the truth is your community's water quality is sub-standard, the perception will take root and then it will become your story, and then it will become your reality. Perception is sometimes the biggest driver of damage to a community, because perception becomes reality. Some of those communities that have experienced illnesses or death due to acute water issues have never fully recovered. Reputations, once acquired, especially those based on horrible and tragic events, are hard to change. When the dominant public perception is that your community is not a good place to live, raise a family and invest in the future that perception will become the reality. Having quality water is no guarantee of success, but having poor water quality is a sure step to failure.

The quality of your water is important to your community's future, but the quantity of water available is equally important. In fact, the issue over the quality of your water is a moot point if you don't have enough water to meet your community's current and future needs. As I mentioned earlier, my grandpa often reminded me you can only survive for three days without water. Adequate water is fundamental to our very survival. Many people in survival situations forget how critically important water is to their bodies, which is why far too many people in survival situations die from dehydration or water poisoning. We also often forget how critical water is to us in our daily lives. We take for granted that it is not only pretty safe to drink, but often presume there is a limitless supply. That is why we let the tap run while we brush our teeth, or let it run until the water is nice and cold for drinking, or water our precious lawns in a drought.

Many of us have experienced water shortages for short or seasonal periods during times of drought. We are all aware of the dangerous situation of a prolonged drought as experienced in California. It can be frustrating when we cannot water our lawns or wash our cars when we want to, but it can be frightening when we become aware there might not be enough water to produce basic electricity, or even enough to drink. Many of us are well aware of how there will be increased competition for water use between those who produce our food, those who produce our energy, and those who produce our goods. Battles over water between industries, between communities, between regions and between nations are on the rise.

Food is critical to our very survival, but food doesn't grow if we don't have water. Every farmer knows how important it is to take good care of the soil. They can pick the best seeds, put them at the right depth, put on the right fertilizers, spray the right chemicals to control weeds and pests and still, if there is no water from rain or irrigation, you know what farmers get — nothing. And neither will you. Value-added agriculture requires vast amounts of water. Manufacturing and industrial activities require water. Tourism initiatives are more successful near water. Everything needs water. In fact, there are many communities around North America that cannot grow larger because there isn't enough water to support growth. People want to buy a plot, build a house, work and volunteer, spend money and raise their families in a community, but they can't because there is not enough water to supply new homes. The problem in many cases is not a shortage of water. The problem is a shortage of water management. Our policies very rarely encourage grey- water technologies or encourage conservation, yet our future access to sufficient water supplies will depend on such policies being put in place now.

In many places the water resources we have available are becoming taxed or maxed. I don't mean the water now has a tax on it, though that may occur someday in some jurisdictions. What I mean is traditional water sources around North America are either beginning to fall under serious strain (taxed) or else they are utilized to their full potential now and can't give another drop (maxed). This situation makes for urgent quantity-of-water concerns our communities must address sooner rather than later. In some places within North America, such issues are pairing up with the inability of communities to find qualified people to ensure quality control measures are in place for their local water supply. This is leading to investments in regional water systems of varying sizes. Such systems provide a higher level of water-quality security, but also make possible the implementation of water-management measures that address quantity and use issues. In the long run forward-looking communities are recognizing such secured access can help enable their community's long-term success and viability.

In a particular community that seemed determined to guarantee its failure the residents worked very hard to fight any and all attempts to link into a regional water system that would give access to large volumes of quality water. Almost a decade earlier the community had realized its water capacity was in jeopardy. It drilled two new wells to supply the community with water but found those wells did not produce the volumes they would need in the future and did not have the quality required by law. Of course they could treat the water, but given the growing age and limited capacity of their water treatment facility, that would require a massive investment in the near future. Their current wells were experiencing reduced capacity. They needed to do something soon. It was fortunate a regional water system was being built that would go right by the community. They were invited to tie into the system if they wanted. It would mean huge supplies of quality water, with no more requirements to hire trained and qualified staff to manage the local water-treatment facility, and no required investment in a new facility. Of course, tying into the line meant all water use, every house and building, would have a meter and have to pay for its water use. Besides the initial infrastructure investment required by the community, metering and billing was how the system and the water would be paid for.

You might expect the solution to such a series of challenges would be obvious, or at least if the solution wasn't obvious then the fact *something* needed to be done would be apparent — but not to this community. There arose three different factions. One faction wanted to tie into the regional water line as part of a long-term solution to the community's problems. A second faction hated the neighboring communities and wanted to remain independent, so they were determined to build a very expensive water-treatment facility and to continue to hire local people to manage the water-quality issues. The third faction wanted neither option, and thought doing nothing was the best plan. The third faction became the loudest and the angriest of the voices. It is important to mention there was actually a fourth group in this three-way debate. They were and always are the largest group, but they aren't a faction. They are the general, and generally disinterested, public-at-large. For the most part they aren't engaged in the details of the discussion and are simply busy with running their businesses or jobs, coaching soccer or hockey, volunteering at the school or for community organizations, and putting away the chairs at church. They typically don't get very engaged, though they are the most impacted by the results of the debate.

When the fourth group did listen at public meetings and in the coffee shops, the third faction held the most sway. In fact, the third faction, the naysayer team, nearly always has the most sway in any debate. I recall watching an argument between two colleagues of mine. The first person was passionate about an idea, and the second believed just as passionately the other fellow was wrong. Their voices got louder and louder until they were both yelling. Another colleague interrupted the argument and calmly said with a sarcastic grin on his face, "Brad (the naysayer) wins because he is the loudest and he is the angriest." I learned that day we often mistake someone being loud and angry for being right. We also often give more credence to the critics than they deserve. It is easy to sound smart when all you have to do is critique other people's actions. And so, in the community debating the solution to the water-supply issue, as the first two factions each presented their case through public meetings, the third faction ran each argument down and made the other groups look foolish. By default the naysayers got what they wanted. They wanted nothing to happen, and by running down every idea for action, all that was left was inaction. The critics fight, and the generally disinterested public-at-large doesn't want to get into a fight with them or be the next targets of those critics, so they give them the win. When you don't exactly know what is going on, you also tend to side with those who are angriest since our primitive instincts whisper in our ear there must be a legitimate reason for them to be angry. *A wrong must exist and they are trying to stop it*, we think. *We should side with them. Besides, I don't want them to get mad at me next. I don't have time for their rage.*

The third faction in this case argued that either of the investment options required too much capital outlay, even when the investments were shown to be very affordable over the life of the infrastructure, while doing nothing would cost the community its future. The third faction argued most families and seniors in the community couldn't afford to pay the cost of a monthly water bill based on use, even though most folks paid far more on a monthly cable or satellite TV bill. Sadly, many of this faction were seniors who argued they didn't see the necessity since the water had been good enough for them for decades, or they didn't want the investment made because they wouldn't be around to see the full benefits. No one had the guts to point out to them the community only existed because their forebears had realized they were building a community that would endure beyond their lifetime. They weren't building something for themselves — they were building for their kids and grandkids and generations to come. It is tough to tell that to some seniors today who will remind you they built this country, as though the job is done and there is no responsibility on the next generation to continue the building. Regardless, for a decade the third faction had their way and nothing happened.

Neighboring communities tied into the new regional water line. Those communities had a new source of abundant quality water. Those communities attracted new families, new business and new industries. New developers created new subdivisions for the new families and new Main Street projects accommodated large volumes of new shoppers in those new businesses. Some of the communities got new schools to accommodate the influx of new students and one community got a new hospital. All of those communities succeeded in attracting new doctors, new professionals who opened new businesses and new government grants to support the infrastructure projects needed to accommodate the new growth. Each community that tied into the new water line underwent a renewal. The one that didn't tie in, however, didn't grow. It shrank. It suffered horribly for an entire decade, but still the community fought the tie-in, and the third faction, whom I affectionately called "Team Angry," continued to win.

Petitions can have a powerful effect on a lot of elected people, but they never worked on me. As a rule of thumb, for every 100 signatories on a petition there will be one real person with true awareness and concern for the issue. In an email writing campaign, 30 identical form-letter emails are equivalent to one informed person who really cares about the issue. When I was an elected official, one phone call to my office from a real person (not associated with a lobby) was representative of 20 real people concerned about the issue. One personal letter written to me from a constituent (not associated with a lobby group) was a measure of 30 real people with deep concern for the issue. The reason for giving personal calls or letters such serious attention was that they usually meant many other people were feeling the same way but had not chosen to call or write to me about their viewpoints. Petitions, on the other hand, are often signed by people who don't really know the details of the issue or sometimes don't even know what it is they are signing.

After many years of watching the community suffer with their water issues I actually thought the tide had started to turn and they would tie in to the water line. Team Angry must have thought so too, so they organized a petition and got almost 1000 signatures. Third factions typically use petitions to enhance their numbers. In reality they are usually a small group right from the beginning, which is why they have to yell so hard, be so angry and take advantage of petitions to gain leverage. In this case I was lucky enough to be presented with a copy of the petition, since I was the champion of rural communities at the time. With far less political grace than I am sure they were accustomed to I tossed it back immediately, telling them it was an embarrassing declaration of stupidity and it was killing the community. I even laid out information for them about how the other communities were succeeding and growing. It didn't matter to them. They were Team Angry and I was their new opponent. I ignored their protests and eventually they faded away. Eventually, the town did connect to the regional system, but they missed many of the great growth opportunities that had come to the region and to the other communities in those early years.

As we close out this chapter I want you to consider a few important and little-known facts. Water covers more than 70 percent of the Earth's surface. It seems abundant to us when we look at the big blue ball on which we live, but less than 2.5 percent of the world's water is fresh water. The rest is saline or unfit for human consumption, and therefore not readily available or useful to us for most purposes. Even more alarming is that less than one percent of the world's water is fresh *and accessible.* That means of all the fresh water that exists in the world, which is only 2.5 percent of all the world's water, only 40 percent of that is even accessible to us. So, in summary, the only water really available for use by the seven billion people on earth amounts to one percent of all the water in the world. Makes you want to turn off the tap while you brush your teeth rather than sending it down the drain and to the ocean where it become saline and unusable, no? The poorest 20 percent of the global population spend more than 10 percent of their income on water. If you had to spend 10 percent of your income on water, how much would that be? The majority of us spend more on television than we do on water, yet we cry foul and misdeed when we have to spend two percent of our income on something we simply cannot survive without. Fully one-sixth of the world's population does not have access to clean drinking (potable) water. That's well over one billion people who don't have access to clean water. The World Health Organization says at any one time half the world's population has one of the six diseases caused by drinking poor-quality water. None of us should take our water quality, or the quantity of it, for granted.

I believe the next Great War will be fought over oil. I also believe the Last Great War fought will be fought over water, because whoever controls the water will control everything. If you think the quality or quantity of water available to your community isn't important, have a second thought. That water coming out of your tap isn't going to guarantee your success, but having poor-quality water will leave your community to drink from a poisoned well, and the lack of quantity will leave your community with an insatiable thirst. Either way, forgetting about your water is a sure way to kill your community.

CHAPTER 2
DON'T ATTRACT BUSINESS

A second way to make sure your community is destined for failure is to be certain you don't attract new businesses or retain businesses you already have. Enticing measures you must avoid at all cost could include competitive business-tax rates, appropriate support services, reduced rules and regulations, flexible multi-use zoning, and an environment friendly to enterprise. But ensuring failure does not mean you don't attract needed businesses to your community — it *especially* means making sure you don't attract businesses that will compete with current businesses owned by you or your friends.

Traveling to so many communities over the years has afforded me the perfect opportunity to ask a lot of questions and collect information and anecdotal stories on community performance in various sectors and over a range of issues. There was obviously a prevalence of communities that said they *wanted* businesses and industries to locate in their community. Few of them realized their policies, taxes and attitudes were operating counter to their stated desire. One mayor said it best: "We thought we were open for business. We even advertised we were, but when we looked at how we operated, we had made it impossible for businesses to move into town."

Some communities hire economic development officers and then abandon them. The EDO works hard to attract business, yet every time they get close to success their own employer — the community — makes decisions and policies that run counter to the goal for which the EDO is hired. Other communities take the smart step of identifying a list of businesses the community needs to have, but then put the list in a binder on a shelf in the town office and simply wait, as though the mere production of a list no one knows about is all that needs to be done to attract business. Most communities seem to genuinely want to do something. They simply don't recognize what needs to be done or where to start the process, and they lack the commitment to see it through with action.

In cases like this I have always advised it is best to develop a list of businesses and services needed in the community. A great place to begin the development of a list of needed businesses is with the current businesses already operating in your community. Most businesses require complementary businesses and services to help them operate and can advise about what might be missing in town that could make their own business run more effectively. For instance, carpenters are often drawn to a town with a hardware store, and a hardware store is always more successful in a town with carpenters. Existing businesses also have had the experience of setting up and operating within your community, so they will be able to advise you on what challenges there may be with taxes, regulations, zoning, labor and so forth creating barriers to new businesses locating in your community. I always mention how important attitude is to the success of your community and business owners will be able to comment firsthand about the impact of negative prevailing attitudes and how they kill your business climate.

The second place to gather input on the businesses your community needs is from residents who have a firsthand account of what types of businesses and services they would like to see added to their community. They know what businesses are available since they probably utilize them, and they know what is lacking since they have to travel outside the community in order to get those services or products. Of course, what people *think* they want and what they *truly need* can often be completely different. A good way to learn the real needs of the community is to conduct a simple survey, not of what people want but of what they actually leave town to purchase. Compile and sort the list into the most common goods and services not available in your community. This will give you the clearest sense of what people truly need, rather than a simple run-down list of what they say they want. The challenge with most communities is figuring out the first step, but once you have a list of what you need, often a clear strategy naturally evolves that can fill in those business gaps.

One of the challenges to a community's success, as I have said before, is its inability to recognize — or perhaps it's a fear of realizing — its success rests entirely within itself. As such, most communities are compelled to find solutions from outside their boundaries. That isn't a bad thing, at least not necessarily. Hiring outside consultants to view a situation has advantages, seeking outside investors has payoffs and implementing outside ideas can cause beneficial change. Looking outside the walls, however, is not always necessary. When it comes to attracting business and service industries to a community, most communities look exclusively outside for those investments. They write letters to corporate head offices asking them to consider opening a store in their town. They run an advertisement or host an open house in some other place to showcase their hometown opportunities. They put up signage inviting out-of-town businessmen to investigate investment and development opportunities. To attract new businesses to open in your community, it is not always necessary that an outsider takes the leap.

I wish communities would take that highway sign facing incoming traffic and turn it around so it faces locals instead. It should read, "Hey, where are you going? Did you know we are open for business? If we don't have what you are looking for here, did you consider there may be an exciting business opportunity since 20 other people left this morning to drive to another town to get/do the same thing you are doing right now? And guess what, we have 10 business owners who could also use that service who have pooled some money and have a low-interest loan available to get you started and grow our community in the process!" OK, maybe that is a really big sign, but you get the point. With a little bit of information on what people leave town for, there may be some local resident who just needs a little push or a little support to open that business or provide that service.

A few communities I have come across have proved to be models of success in this regard. In one example, several ranchers got together and more importantly put some money together, to build a veterinary clinic. The community didn't have such a clinic, but they recognized they needed one. The local business owners threw in financial and moral support because they realized ranchers and pet owners traveling to a different town to see a vet would also stop at the other town's hardware store, the restaurant, and sometimes the grocery store, thus taking revenue away from their own community. So they sought and found a young veterinarian with good experience who was seeking an opportunity to own his own clinic and new business. The group offered him a low-interest loan and made it clear he and his family were wanted in the community over the long-term. It was what every great business venture starts out as — complementary interests meeting complementary needs. The ranchers and the small business owners realized the entire town was suffering because of the lack of a vet in the community. They realized *they* had a problem and *they* had to fix it.

Business members and the council of another community pooled funds and collectively bought some housing properties located in a larger community between a trade college and a university where many of their young people went off to school. They offered contracts for free accommodations to students in the region if they were taking a program, either trade or profession, identified as being needed by the region. In return, the students signed a contract obliging them to remain or return to the region upon graduation to provide services for a pre-established period of time. If there weren't enough local students who signed up for contracts they would offer the same deal of free accommodations to students from outside the area on the condition they too would stay in the region for a stipulated period of time following graduation. The civic and business leaders in the region reported to me new industries have sprung up because of the available skilled labor supply, new businesses have opened because of the increased population and economic activity and the number of professional services has increased to a point where more people come to town for services than leave to get services. Welders, carpenters, plumbers, dental hygienists, nurse aides, opticians and optometrists, teachers, one doctor, a hardware store and an oilfield service and supply business have all opened. Even their own well-qualified town manager came from this investment.

The success of your community relies on attracting new businesses, but it is just as important to be certain your policies, taxes, regulations and such are designed to retain existing businesses — otherwise, neither the ones you have, nor the ones you draw in, are going to stay for very long. Yet there are many communities that offer incentives to attract new businesses to the community but do nothing to keep existing businesses strong and healthy. It is much like the stories we have heard, or the experiences we have had, with cellular phone or cable companies offering new customers an incentive to join, but offering nothing to the loyal, dedicated customers who have been with them on a long-standing basis. The two groups don't have to be offered the exact same supports because they have different needs and motivations, but you need to demonstrate an appreciation for both new and existing businesses. Not doing so will earn your community a reputation as a place that may be good for new business, but not for businesses that are already operating there. Few people want to invest in a community known to start things off well, which then turns against them later. So if you want to kill your community you must drive out your existing businesses by ensuring they don't have a competitive tax rate or fair business costs, are encumbered by costly and burdensome rules and regulations, don't get the services they require to operate and operate in an anti-business community environment.

There is something that is even more important, however, if you are going to drive out business as part of your campaign to guarantee failure. I need you to read closely and bear with me through this part because it is going to sound counter-intuitive and quite possibly absurd. To drive businesses out of business, to cause businesses to go broke and fail, you must ensure they have no competition within the community. Let that soak in for a moment. Yes, if the businesses within your community have no competition you will help secure their failure, and ultimately the failure of your community. I found many wonderful examples of this wherever I traveled, but in few places was it as starkly displayed and vividly observed as with local grocery stores.

I traveled to a lot of communities with populations in the range of 800 to 2000 people. I identified communities of almost identical size, and in comparing them found little reason why some would have two grocery stores while the others of virtually the same size would have only one grocery store. The population of the communities and the surrounding areas wasn't a factor, since they were the same, so I explored what other factors could cause the critical tipping point that would encourage a second grocery store to open in some communities, but not others. Could it be the foundation of the local economy? Perhaps it was a unique, short-term opportunity that had generated the second store and it simply remained open. Perhaps it was a historical context — if you had two stores generations ago, you always had two, but if you had one, you always had one. It turned out none of those were the cause.

I began conducting more in-depth unofficial interviews with grocery store owners to see if they could provide some insight, and I discovered something I hadn't been expecting. In a community with one grocery store, the owner almost always confirmed they were having a very tough time just getting by, yet in a comparable-sized community with two grocery stores the owners confirmed although they weren't going to become millionaires they were making a pretty good living. In fact, I found plenty of examples of two grocery store owners in towns of 1000 who were both successful, yet single grocery store owners in communities of 1500 who were not. This was counter-intuitive on a grand scale. For a thought experiment let us use two towns of 1000 people each, one having one grocery store and the other having two. Our business intuition says the store owner with exclusive jurisdiction over the 1000 potential customers would have to be more successful than the two grocery store owners who are forced to share the market of 1000 residents. It should be just that simple, no? What is being overlooked in those cases and turned out to be the chief cause of why two grocery stores in a community could find success but a single one couldn't, was the value competition brings to the community and to the businesses.

We all see, know and preach the value of competition. We know competition is good for the economy because it advances performance on four key aspects: price, quality, selection and service. Those four key aspects are important to consumers, who often make their spending choices based on achieving a sense of value in some combination of those four key aspects. Competition helps keep the price of goods and services low. Competition ensures we get better- quality products. Competition gets us better levels of service. Competition delivers us a greater variety of products and services matching our interests and desires. Nations where competition is not embraced, such as the pre-Cold War-era USSR, are stellar examples of how the lack of competition ensures consumers pay high prices for poor products, limited selection and dismal service. Without competition there is no incentive to improve and without an incentive to improve, frankly, improvement doesn't occur.

We too often simplify the benefit and value of competition down to just getting the best price for the goods we want to purchase. Competition is not always about price, though. In fact, it seems to be less and less about price because we as consumers don't place as much emphasis as we used to on low price as the determining factor of a purchase. Granted, there are low price providers aplenty, but there are more companies than ever choosing not to be the low-cost supplier because margins are so slim. Instead they are looking to offer a product that drives a high willingness to pay. They do so by offering a better quality, a more innovative, or a more personalized array of products. Some focus on the service level they can provide with their products. Mottos about how businesses have the best service, or the most choice and variety, or the quality you can trust, abound everywhere. Indeed, some companies have been incredibly successful linking their brand name to just one of the above selling points. Once we have bought into one of those other competition drivers, the price point is often much less of an issue. Competition is not simply about price.

Returning to our grocery store thought-experiment, we discover that the single grocery store in a community, regardless of its size, has no open competition to drive its business model, if it even uses a business model. Why would you need a business model when you are the only game in town? There is no incentive to work on offering great pricing. Mark everything up as high as you want, because there is no one else in town to buy the product from, right? Why offer service with a smile? Who cares if we smile since no one could shop here more often than they already do and they have nowhere else to go if we don't — we are the only game in town, remember? Improve quality? Offer more variety? "No way. Hey, you get what I get when I bring it in, and until then we have what we have." Without competition there is no drive to improve or to compete for dollars that could go across the street.

The other community, the one with two grocery stores and the same population, has competition. This means each must compete to do better than the other guy down the street. They compete by offering a better price, higher quality, more diverse selection, or better service. It is a fact of life that no single person can be all things to all people, and the same is true of business. Each business is going to find it does better than the competition in some areas, and falls behind in other areas. Successful businesses choose what they want to excel at and put their energies there. In my travels through communities I've heard people say, "I go to that grocery store because they have the best prices on the canned goods, but I go to the other one because they always have the best quality cuts of meat." Or I've heard them say, "I go to that grocery store because they have the most diverse selection of produce, but I go to the other one because young men carry my bags out to the car for me." Everyone had their different reasons for their shopping habits, and each store was always better at some things than the others. Those comments were the sweet sound of competition doing its work for consumers.

Competition also helped the businesses be more successful because the competition encouraged more dollars to be spent in town rather than outside the community. In the community with one grocery store, where consumers did not get the value of competition, the owner was fortunate to get half of the 1000 people who lived in the town to do business with him. Most of the townsfolk left to spend their money in a place where they got the benefits of competition. Where did they go? They went down the road to the community with two grocery stores to take advantage of the benefits of their competition. The two grocery store owners in the same town didn't just share the 1000 members of their own community, but shared shoppers from out of town who came in looking for the benefits of competition caused by having two grocery stores.

It took a while for me to see it was competition that was driving the success of those small-town groceries, and the lack of it that was driving failure in the other town. I wasn't the only one who failed to see the connection. The owner of that single grocery store would always tell me he or she and their family, could barely make a living in the town so there was absolutely no need for another competing grocery store in the community. At first blush it would definitely appear that way. In reality, however, competition is what drives us to be successful and is an element critical to our communities' success. It is critical if people are going to feel they are getting value when they spend their money, and it is critical if they are going to spend their money in the community. We all understand the value of competition, we all praise the benefits of competition and we all welcome competition — up until the moment we are the ones who are being competed against.

In one community there was an entrepreneur who wanted to open a franchise gas station because he thought it would be a good business for himself and would be beneficial to the community. Excited, the young entrepreneur went to the town administration seeking to buy land and have it zoned appropriately, to apply for the requisite development permits and building permits, and arrange to address any other issues he had not foreseen. He had no idea he would have such troubles. Road block after road block was tossed in front of him by the administration. After more than six months of getting nowhere and not having his calls even returned any more, he gave up. He moved an hour down the highway to another community and had his land bought, zoned, and permitted, and the business up and running in less than a year. When he relayed that story to me I simply had to go back to his hometown to find out what had happened. Although he couldn't understand why he was treated as he was, it turns out everyone else knew quite well why that young entrepreneur's gas station business was stalled by the town. Everyone openly told me it was because the mayor at the time owned the only other gas station in town, across the highway from where the young man wanted to build, and the mayor didn't want the competition.

Interestingly, many residents said they didn't buy gas in the community. The mayor's gas station was the only one in town so he charged an exorbitant price thanks to his virtual monopoly. The extra high price for gasoline was commonly referred to as the "mayor's gas tax," not because it was a tax imposed by council, but because it was a premium imposed by the mayor, who used his position to keep out any competition. Many people would drive almost 30 minutes to another community to avoid paying the premium charged on gas, and would then also buy groceries and hardware supplies and so on, while they were there. I will address that situation in more depth in Chapter 5. Unquestionably, a little competition over the gas price would have been healthy for the community and would have kept money in town with local businesses.

Three years later in the same community the town had elected a new mayor. The real problem remained, however, as another entrepreneur discovered when he tried to open an auto parts specialist store. That entrepreneur experienced many of the same roadblocks the previous entrepreneur did. Roadblock after roadblock appeared, until finally the entrepreneur took the business to a neighboring community only thirty minutes away and set up shop in less than a year. Again, people were very open in talking about the situation and freely admitted the challenge at that time was the new mayor who was the manager of a competing auto parts store and didn't want the competition. I couldn't believe this could happen twice in back-to-back cases in such a short span in the same community. The longer I stayed, however, the more I learned just how fast the crazy ran in that community. I began to feel like a Catholic priest at Sunday confession. Everyone had a story about how the community had chased away business.

The women who served as the town secretary for over 25 years confessed to me that for her entire career there had been fresh streams of entrepreneurial welders knocking on the town's door, looking to buy industrial land so they could open welding shops. She admitted to using her position as the first point of contact within the town office to do everything in her power to encourage them to go away. She would say there was no more industrial land for sale, or that it was contaminated. She would say the school was horrible, the town was infested with drugs, the economy was dying, or the taxes would break them. She would say anything she could to get them to go away. Why? Her husband was a welder and they didn't want the competition. There are thousands of examples of incidents like that in communities across North America and indeed your community probably has some stories of its own, whether you know about them or not.

But let us remember the subject of this book is how to make your community fail. Killing your community means you must make sure it has no thriving business sector. In order to achieve that you will need to eliminate all policies, regulations, or plans in place to attract any new businesses. New businesses bring investment and money, encourage local shopping and create new jobs, which just reinforces and strengthens your economy.

Even if no new businesses are attracted to your community it probably has a potentially strong base of existing businesses on which to build success. This cannot be tolerated. You must work hard to eliminate competitive business tax rates, freedom from excessive rules and regulations, and an environment friendly to business enterprises. If that still doesn't work you must also drive away any business that would compete with other local businesses. That will ensure customers must leave to get good price, quality, selection and service, and you will be left with a wonderful little monopoly . . . on failure.

CHAPTER 3
DON'T ENGAGE YOUTH

Please don't confuse youth with kids. When I refer to "youth" I mean anyone approximately 35 years and younger. They are typically the most energetic individuals within your community, full of creative, innovative ideas, but not yet prejudiced by bad experiences and fruitless pursuits. Within youth lies the hope anything is still possible if we can just dream it. They also have the energy and passion to pursue those dreams to their realization. If you wish to eliminate any future for your community you must be vigilant in snuffing out those hopes and dreams; the energy and passion, which are naturally bound up in those visionary packages we call youth roaming your community. You must be certain that young people are not part of your councils, your chambers, your volunteer organizations or any committee where that energy or those ideas might find life. It is of critical importance, if you are going to kill your community, to be sure those youth do not become engaged and active participants in community life. If you are skillful, their energy and ideas will die and your town can be killed with them. If you are *really* skillful, the persistent ones will leave town, taking all that energy and all those ideas with them, and you can rest assured the hope they embody won't rise from the grave to spoil your plans for certain failure.

A call to action for ensuring failure is to avoid implementing any type of succession planning in your community. This is especially important in communities that depend largely on agriculture. Given the nature of the agriculture economy there are many programs available all across North America that offer free tax-succession planning advice to farmers looking to pass the farm on to the next generation. Regardless of where you farm, if you don't appropriately plan for succession you not only risk giving a significant portion of the farm to the government by way of taxes, you also risk having very little of the farm left to pass on to your children. However, succession planning is not only important to the couple who wishes to retire from farming, or to the next generation wishing to step in and take over the farm, but is also critically important to the integrity and future of communities built primarily upon agricultural economies.

Succession planning is important for all of our communities, yet I have found very few communities planning for succession in leadership positions as older members approach retirement. I originally believed in every case it was merely an oversight or lack of understanding of the importance of succession planning. I discovered, however, there was often a darker and deeper issue at hand when I actually heard some people express a deliberate desire to keep young people from participating in any sort of leadership or governance roles. I had a community leader come up to me, after I had finished speaking at a community session on engaging youth, and argue those young people should wait like he did until they were over 40 and knew something about life. My reaction was to laugh out loud, as I was sure his comments were in jest. I was wrong. He was completely serious. I am not suggesting all community leaders share his sentiment, but I was astonished anyone thought this, let alone that someone would openly admit it. Listening carefully, I realized the attitude was more prevalent than I had anticipated, and though few expressed those sentiments openly in words, many demonstrated the feelings through actions and behavior. Though this behavior may have been non-deliberate and subconscious, the consequences were the same as if the community leaders had deliberately chosen to exclude youth.

I would have expected those types of comments to be part of a vigorous debate over issues that would affect the future viability of the community. Such debates can obviously ignite passions and cause people to say ridiculous things. Rather, the comments often came at quiet times, which suggested to me there was some underlying level of resentment or hostility toward those youth. Publicly there seemed to be a full understanding and appreciation of the need to educate, engage, and develop those young people into leaders. Privately, there lingered a quiet but recognizable resentment against the opportunities available to, and the youthfulness, of that next generation. It was a classic, but very real, Disney story — the old witch jealous of the vitality and beauty of the young. I had sensed it when I was younger, but now, as an outsider to each community, I was witnessing it firsthand. It was horrendously sad to watch.

I have only ever come across one community doing any succession planning for Main Street businesses. It is so easy to leave succession planning to the businesses themselves to figure out, but if you are concerned about your community's future then the state of your community's businesses, and their succession plans, must be a concern as well. We fret about the future of agriculture when we realize the average age of farmers is over 55, but in many of our small communities the average age of business owners is not much lower. I'm not suggesting you interfere in business owners' retirement plans, but perhaps there is a ripe opportunity for a little broader education about the opportunities for business owners upon retirement, beyond simply closing and locking their front doors. Few of our communities' business owners are planning for someone to take over their business, and even fewer of those have any understanding their best options for transition to a new generation of business owners are sitting right there in the community.

In high school I participated in a course of study called Work Experience. It was a program that partnered businesses with high school students to give the students an academic credit for working and at the same time give them a chance to learn about that business from the owner. My work experience was especially beneficial as I labored throughout the entire program at sweeping floors. Yes, if I am ever looking for a new career or job opportunity I can always fall back on the skill I developed over all those months of sweeping the floor. At the end of the program I found out the majority of my classmates were acquiring much the same experience base as me. Unfortunately that meant we all might find ourselves competing for the same position in the same warehouse one day. That work experience wasn't much of an experience.

I don't blame anyone for the manner in which the program was executed. It was simply that the program lost sight of, or never fully developed into, its full potential. There were a lot of opportunities for business owners who were starting to think about their retirement and thinking of turning the equity in their business into more time on the golf course, or traveling. There were a lot of young people passing through high school wondering what they wanted to be and what they wanted to do with their lives. Many of them had no idea owning their own business was an option, even though if they had learned of that opportunity, they undoubtedly would have found tremendous excitement at the prospect. Personally, I was always under the impression my options were to farm, to work in the oil patch, or to go off to university with the expectation I would never come back.

No one connected me to the opportunities that lay before me within the community. No one showed me what businesses existed with the notion I could eventually own one. No one showed me what businesses were missing and encouraged me to start one of my own someday. No one explained to me that if I wanted to be a doctor, or a dentist, or a lawyer, or a teacher, or a psychologist, or an engineer I could go away to school, and then I could come back to the community where I'd grown up to set up a practice. No one did anything like that for any of the young people getting ready to graduate. Few communities do that for their youth and for the sake of their own community's future, even though we all know our communities are continually in need of new businesses, new business owners, doctors, dentists, teachers, psychologists, engineers and so on.

Over the first 21 years of my life on this Earth my dad convinced me I didn't want to be a farmer. He would say to me, or more often I would hear him say to others; there was no hope or future in farming; you only get one good crop for every seven years of bad ones; and when you have one good crop everyone else has a good one too, so it's not worth anything. Land prices kept going up, equipment costs kept going up, input costs kept going up, but what you had to sell was always worth less and less. Agriculture is a lot of work — a lot of investment with little return, little time for vacations or trips, and a lot of thankless hours. I heard those words over and over from him and other farmers in the area. Of course I would hear these conversations more frequently when times were tough, when we'd had little sleep, or when we were having a bad day, which was often enough, but when times were good I heard very few positive comments spoken by him or the other farmers in the area. I still like to remind my dad, he and our neighbors did a superb job of convincing me that deliberately choosing to be a farmer was a stupid choice. When I returned from university with my first degree, my dad asked me if I was interested in taking over the ranch. I was amazed he had the gall to look surprised when I said, "No."

I will probably anger a few people with these words, but I think it is important to talk about how we have accepted a subconscious mindset that is risking a (sometimes real, sometimes perceived) dumbing-down of agriculture and rural communities. Over generations in agriculture we have developed an unspoken mindset that the smartest children go off to university to do something . . . smart. The less intelligent children have to stay back and . . . farm. The reality is that being a successful farmer takes a lot of brains and business savvy and often now, a university degree. However, we have created this mindset agriculture is for the kids who aren't smart enough for university, and if you stay in farming it's because you weren't able to do something else. It doesn't matter if it's true. We have built up a cultural motif that has dumbed down farming in the eyes of the next generation, and eventually, if the mindset stays, it will become a reality. There is now almost a level of shame in the occupation when really it should be celebrated as a complex and fascinating business that takes a lot of intelligence and people skills. Agriculture is for the smart, the brave, and the visionary, not for the weak and simple-minded, yet that isn't what we communicate to the next generation or the public with our word and deed.

We express much the same mindset for our rural communities. The smart ones are supposed to leave for university and won't, in fact shouldn't, be back. The ones who can't do anything else stay. Are the ones who stay in our communities less intelligent or less hard working? Of course not. How long will it be though, after years and generations of holding onto such a subconscious attitude, before it becomes a reality? Perhaps all the smart youth will leave, eventually. Perhaps the ones who remain will begin to believe they aren't as smart. It doesn't matter which is the case because our attitude eventually creates our reality. Our attitude is threatening to dumb down agriculture and our small rural communities. That will become our reality if we don't turn the tide.

We don't just leave our youth with the idea there are no businesses to build or take over, or there are no new professionals needed in the community. Our youth become convinced, by our own word and deed, that the future is bleak and the only hope lies outside of town. Often we go to great lengths, deliberate or accidental, to convince them staying in the community assures them a lifetime of sweeping floors. I say "accidental" because we simply don't realize the psychological consequence of our constant negativity on impression-able youth. My dad would confess he now realizes the impact those 21 years of complaining had on me, but he didn't deliberately try to talk me out of farming. Farmers complain about how awful farming is and then lament their sons and daughters don't want to farm. We do the exact same thing in our communities. Communities, deliberately or accidently, tell their youth there is no hope in their town, there is no future, and that youth are stupid if they stay. Then they lament when the youth actually do leave.

I was invited to a particular lunch-hour meeting in one community to advise businessmen, political leaders, seniors, youth, volunteers and such on how to build a culture of success in the community. We sat down for lunch and I listened to the conversations around the large circle of tables. One gentleman was engaged in a loud discussion about how the community was shrinking in population as fast as it was shrinking in opportunity. He doubted they would bother to keep the hospital open much longer, (which was patently untrue and he knew it) and he said when that happened all the businesses would just pack up and leave. In short, he was a downer and his reasons for being down had more to do with his temperament than the reality of the community.

I noticed the young people around him listening intently as he described the house of falling cards he imagined was his community. After we finished lunch I did my presentation and then we moved on to questions and answers for the remainder of the lunchtime. I was so enthralled when that negative gentleman was the first to ask a question. He said, "Doug, like every other community of our size, our biggest challenge is that youth keep leaving. How do we get our youth to stay here?" Now, as a former teacher I am well known for my patience and decorum in addressing any question, no matter how ridiculous I believe it to be, so I shocked myself when I simply blurted out, "Shut up!"

I was even more shocked when a round of applause started up. Obviously his negativity had become commonplace and many realized those two simple words were the only answer to such a question. I did apologize to the gentleman. It turned out he was the mayor. I explained to him and everyone else, telling our youth over and over there is no hope or future in your community and then wondering why they leave is ironic to the core. He agreed, but I think he was still angry with me for the embarrassment he felt he suffered. He never did invite me back to town. In the end it was a very good exercise, however, and helped the community purge some very dark demons people were afraid to fight — the reason many youth leave and don't return is because of the negative attitude of the community.

Typically when people ask me how to keep youth in their community I don't tell them to shut up, but I do tell them the notion the community is supposed to keep their youth is entirely wrong. "Keeping" youth in a community sounds like they are being tied to lampposts on Main Street, or roads are being blown up so they can't leave town. You shouldn't try to "keep" your youth. The nature of youth is to explore, to try new things, to seek new adventures. The more they experience of life, or other cultures, or other ways of thinking and doing things, the more creative, more understanding, more thoughtful, and better-rounded they will be. This means they will be better community leaders, better business leaders, and better social leaders replete with broader ideas and concepts they can exercise within your community to help it to grow.

If your youth are not allowed to explore where adventure lurks, they will not learn anything beyond what they are given in the community. This does not mean all youth have to leave and go exploring, or there is something wrong with them if they don't, but if they seek to go, you should not strategize to hold them back. If you try to keep all of the youth in your community you risk developing an entire generation with no experiences and no solutions beyond the town's history, and no vision beyond the town's own water tower. By keeping them all at home there is a great risk of having an entire generation with no outside world experience, who could all too easily become very small-minded and routine, because there is nothing and no one to bring some outside experience or knowledge into the community. When it comes to youth, the future of your community is not about finding a way to keep them from leaving. The future of your community is dependent on providing all of them with a reason to want to come home when the adventure is over.

I found a community that was a fascinating case study of youth engagement. For years, the business and community leaders met with the grade 11 and 12 students and asked them what they were up to and what they were interested in doing with their futures. The town leaders, both council and business, took it upon themselves to create jobs or business opportunities for the next crop of graduates from the local high school. The local business owners invested capital into a business incubator to help entrepreneurial youth with prospective business ideas. Those business leaders developed and governed a fund to loan to youth in the community who were ready to take their idea beyond the incubator stage. They also provided mentorship to those young entrepreneurs and a place they could share successful strategies.

Jobs and business opportunities were created in that community. It was never intended to stop youth from wanting to venture away, but it did assure them they had a place if and when they were ready to return home. They also found an added benefit they had not foreseen. If they created 30 jobs, or professional or business opportunities for 30 youth who were graduating in their community, not all of their youth stayed, but youth from *other* communities did move in. The community had developed a reputation as a place that was welcoming and encouraging for young, entrepreneurial people. The town grew and the average age of the population decreased, counter to what was happening in other similar communities within the region. Their worries turned from their community's future existence to the community's need for infrastructure to handle the new growth pressures. It was a wonderful problem to have.

The success of that community reminded me of wise words I heard from a young woman named Shawna. Shawna was dismayed at how nonchalantly some community leaders discussed the situation they faced with youth in their community. She heard those leaders say, "We can't get youth engaged in our community," or "The youth of the community are leaving and won't be back." They said those words and then simply shrugged their shoulders and shook their heads as though it was just a fact of life, and they were helpless to change the situation. There was no sense of urgency in their voices. They often gave no sense they actually understood how scary the situation was for the community. To change that, Shawna advised them to replace the word "youth" in those statements with the word "future," since youth are the future. That little experiment ended the shoulder-shrugging pretty quickly, and created a sudden understanding of the trouble the community was in. Go ahead — try it yourself. Substitute the words in the statements above and see how it makes you feel. I'll wait.

Pretty powerful, isn't it? "The future of our community is leaving and won't be back." That is scary. Shawna had a couple of other pieces of advice that have proved true. She taught me when an older person asks the younger generation for some help, or to join them in something, the younger folks don't believe the invitation is sincere. When you see the younger generation at a social gathering, a wedding dance, a fundraising dinner, a pancake breakfast or just on the street, do you actually stop to talk to them, or sit with them? Not usually, if ever. If you do, some will probably question your motives, because you don't do it regularly. If you don't do it regularly there is no point in trying, because one engagement without any kind of follow-up will leave them believing you really don't want their input or their help. In their minds, that first or only invitation isn't sincere because you never cared to engage them before and you confirm it by not engaging them again. Truthfully, if you haven't given them evidence you want their help or their involvement before, are you sure you really want them? Perhaps it's a request just to make you feel better because now you can say you tried? You must really intend to engage the younger generation, and stick with it if you expect them to trust you.

If you want the youth to believe you really mean what you say in your attempts to invite them and engage them, as a rule of thumb you have to ask them seven times. It's actually a psychological condition of all people. We are skeptical of most things we hear initially, but after we have heard the same thing seven times we begin to believe even the most ridiculous lies. So, for youth, you have to ask them if they are interested. You have to ask them a second time if they are interested. You have to stop them on the street and talk to them about what is happening in their lives if you want them to take you seriously. You need to fill your fundraising table with young couples instead of old friends. You need to get up from the table full of the usual suspects and join the youth at the next pancake breakfast if you expect them to accept your invitation to your next group meeting or function. Don't get discouraged if they don't take you seriously the first time. You have to ask them seven times before they think you mean it. If you don't believe me just ask any parent of a teenager how many times they have to ask their son or daughter to take out the garbage before they actually seem to pay attention and take it out. It's seven times.

Shawna also taught me there are three levels of youth engagement. It doesn't matter what the organization is, these three levels will invariably apply. The first level of engagement, or more appropriately the lack thereof, is to invite youth in for consultation and to ask them what they perceive as problems or challenges within the community, group, or organization you are trying to fix. Once the youth have identified those, the usual procedure is that you dismiss them and begin to work on your own solutions to the problems and challenges they have identified. "Thank you for identifying the challenges, and we assure you we now have our best people working on the solutions." Typically this scenario is orchestrated with the intent of making a group feel as though they have been consulted and listened to, but there is very little real commitment to actually resolve the challenges identified. Youth may be inexperienced but they aren't so naive as to think anything meaningful will come of this type of consultation.

The second, and more meaningful, level of engagement occurs when consultation involves an identification of the challenges or problems, but also an identification of assorted potential solutions. You essentially invite youth to lay out the challenges and what they envision are potential solutions. You and your organization, not the youth, then evaluate the solutions proposed and choose what to implement and how to implement it. This, however, still misses the critical element of true engagement. That element is the hardest thing for people in positions of power to master — the ability to let go of that power from their hands.

The third way to engage youth, and frankly any other group, is much like the previous levels. You ask for them to identify challenges like in level one, you ask them to identify solutions like in level two, but in level three, you also give then power and responsibility for implementing the solutions. You give them ownership of the implementation and responsibility for the results. To have true legitimacy and to effect the most change possible, you have got to turn some power and responsibility over to those young people so they themselves can make the necessary changes. It is difficult for people in a position of authority to turn over power, but often to get full and meaningful engagement, to create the leaders of tomorrow you so desperately need to have today, you must give those youth a chance to take leadership roles, and to learn responsibility.

But let us not forget, of course, our real mission is to kill our community, not contribute to its salvation. It is critical, therefore, you take every possible step to avoid engaging your youth. They are your future business owners, professionals and trades people who can set down roots, build families and build your community. So shrink their worlds. Push them into a corner where they feel unneeded, unwanted, and unvalued, so they don't get involved, don't gain experience and have no ability to take the reins from you, at least until they are over 40. Free-minded, brave, or wise souls should be pushed right out of town, taught to forget the way home, and convinced never to return by teaching them they have no future in your community. If you do this successfully you will ensure your youth aren't there when you need them. You can ensure those who left will never return home. You can ensure the ones who remain are able to sweep away the last remnants of hope. With no youth, you can ensure your community has no future.

CHAPTER 4
DECEIVE YOURSELF

Every single community that exists has strengths and weaknesses. From the largest city to the smallest village, every community has elements that draw people to want to call it home, even though it may remain something less than utopia. A community's strengths make up the collective competitive advantage it has over others. It may be the natural landscape or the weather, it may be the culture and the services, it may be the arts and entertainment, or it may be its people and how they treat each other. Regardless, each and every community has some attractive features that have drawn people to move there or stay there. Likewise, every single community has some features about it that are not so appealing and create a specific disadvantage in comparison to other communities. The key to failure is to remain blind to what makes you great and what makes you weak. In essence, failure means being deliberately ignorant about who you are and what you can be.

My grandpa used to tell me understanding what people are thinking and why they act the way they do is easy if you identify the lies they tell themselves. If you listen closely, people will almost always reveal what those lies are, even though they aren't consciously aware of them. Don't be too judgmental. We all have lies we tell ourselves. They are the stories we create in our minds to explain the way the world works. They aren't true, but they make it easier for us to understand the way things around us happen and to cope with events and people that may hurt us. Few of us are brave enough to find out what our own lies are because they leave our egos exposed to realities hard to endure and difficult to accept. They are what we believe, or perhaps more appropriately, what we need to believe, in order for the world to make sense to us: "I am a genius, but the world is stupid so they don't understand me, and that is why they don't recognize my genius." Perhaps that is true and you are a misunderstood genius. The alternative is you really aren't a genius at all. One is a lie that explains away the way the world treats us, while the other is a hard-to-accept truth.

It certainly is easier to believe the world is wrong rather than you are wrong. When our own lies are challenged we react with anger, because the foundation of how we understand the world is being challenged and at risk of being overturned. Exposing our lies forces us to look inward with honesty, leading to a deeper understanding of who we are, which then leads us to recognize our own power to change the world, and ourselves, as necessary. However, creating a false reality that leaves blame and fault at the world's feet is much easier, so we carry on believing our own lies. When our lies are confirmed by someone, that person often becomes our friend. If that friend no longer supports us in the lies we tell ourselves, that person often becomes unfriended. Our lies make us feel better about ourselves and are a way of saying, "I don't need to change. It's not me who has the problem. I'm right. It is 'they' who are wrong. They are the ones who need to change." Those are lies. All lies.

Communities tell themselves lies too, and for the same reasons people do. A community will lie to itself about what it is and why it is the way it is, because doing so is easier than doing something about it. It is easier to point the blame elsewhere than it is to honestly see why the community is really failing and how it could change its fortunes. It may lie to itself about what it is. "We are a strong prosperous city," it says, as its downtown core empties and poverty and crime rates grow. It will obviously attribute any information that is counter to its claim about who it is to forces beyond its control. It may pretend to be something it is not. "We are a progressively environmental city," it says, as it changes vehicle lanes to bicycle lanes in a climate frozen and under a foot of snow seven months of the year, rendering a large stretch of infrastructure underutilized while idling vehicles in the remaining long-congested vehicle lanes compound environmental impacts. Regardless, like people, communities lie to themselves about their reality. They create fictitious stories to explain away what doesn't work or fit into that story they tell themselves. Just as for people, the lies don't serve them very well, and the longer they hold onto the lies, the tougher it is to let them go.

I have often been called a community therapist for the work I do. Though we have a lot of valuable tools to help communities, not every community needs a therapist. There are a couple of processes communities can try themselves, which will reveal the real state of affairs in the community and begin to loosen the bonds of self-deception. I recommend something I have dubbed the "two-list" exercise. This is the first step to assist your collective community to see what is good about itself and what needs to be fixed. The second step is a straightforward character assessment. I used to call this a values assessment, but far too many communities delve right into a description of what they believe to be their moral character, which is frankly not all that useful, and most communities simply carry on with the lies anyway. A character assessment is intended to help you identify those attributes, good and bad, that define who you are.

The "two-list" exercise is very straightforward. I always recommend the exercise begin by collecting a small group of people (more than seven but less than 20, where 13 is the ideal number in my mind for obvious reasons). Those individuals need to be the people of influence within the community, not necessarily the people of power. Apologies to those in power, whose egos may be hurt, but such people are often neck-deep in the day-to-day survival of the community or embroiled in political issues. Sometimes they are in place simply because of their surname, a willingness to serve, or political savvy. Sometimes they are too comfortably set in the status quo, or are too busy with the tyranny of the urgent to embrace change. Their position does not guarantee they have a strong influence over the community. More often than not they are forced to respond to the community, more than they get to lead it. Initiating this exercise with a room comprised entirely of people of power is the best way to be certain nothing gets done. Keep your focus on the people of influence. That does not mean you exclude the people of power. If someone is a person of influence *and* a person of power that is wonderful and amazing. Include them. Always remember, however, if you want to be successful in your endeavors, identify the people of influence and gather them together.

The second step is to give that assembled group two simple questions a couple of days in advance of the meeting. Ask them to consider, "What do we have that makes our community great?" and "What things in our community need to be fixed?" These are easy, straightforward questions. When the invited folks arrive for the meeting, have them put their answers together and rank them. For the list of "what makes the community great," rank the answers from most underappreciated asset to the best recognized. For the list of "what needs to be fixed," have them rank the answers as challenges from the easiest to fix to the hardest to address. That is it. Now turn those people of influence loose and watch them go to work — because that is what people of influence do.

I presented this option to a community several years ago and they took my advice to the letter, and then took it a couple of steps further. When they had developed the lists, they proceeded to put them up in the town office. The list of all great things about the community was put up in a very visual location so all of the public who came into the office could see it clearly. Remember, at the top of the list were the most underappreciated but wonderful aspects of the community. It was reported to me that people would look at the list and openly comment about how they had forgotten the community had that great feature or asset, which other communities didn't have. The people of influence talked as well. Word began to spread about the list; about the list of great things, and what was on that list. The community at large began to talk about the great aspects they had taken for granted for so long. They began to talk about all of the positives. As one person said to me, "We began to celebrate what made us great." Word spread through the community and word spread beyond the community. Soon other communities were talking about what made the community great. It was powerful and it was positive, and most importantly, it changed attitudes.

The second list ranking what needed to be fixed in the community was equally effective, but for different reasons. The organizers of that original meeting didn't know what to do with the second list so they put it up in the back room of the town office until they could decide how to handle it. The interesting thing about the people of influence is they talk to so many others in the community, and this time was no exception. What was on the list became a topic of discussion around the community. Within two weeks a couple of gentlemen showed up at the office and asked to see the list of things that needed to be fixed. The item at the top of the list was considered to be the easiest, since they were already ranked that way. The two gentlemen fixed the first item on the list that weekend. It was a small project — it was easy, and according to the two gentlemen and a third who joined them, it was also fun to do. They visited and laughed and felt good about what they had accomplished. One of them was thrilled he had avoided cleaning the garage because he was helping the community out.

The following week the three gentlemen showed up to tackle the next project on the list. Again, it was a relatively easy project and they enjoyed themselves in completing it. The following week they showed up to tackle the third item on the list, but they actually had to move down to the fifth project because two other groups had shown up to tackle the third and fourth projects already. Word was spreading and small groups were signing up to tackle easy projects. More groups formed and the groups got larger and more confident. Soon there were items on the list the community never would have believed they could handle or resolve. The community at large began to believe there was no challenge they could not overcome together. They bragged about it around town, and they bragged about it outside of town to the point other communities began to talk about what the community was capable of. Again, it was powerful and it was positive, and again, it changed attitudes.

The community developed a sense of pride and confidence in itself as it had success after success, and it began to celebrate what made it great. It acquired the reputation that it valued what it had, and had a willingness to fix what ailed it. The community grew. New businesses entered the town, new families moved in and new developments sprung up. The community became the happening place because it acquired a reputation as the place where things happen. The "two-list" exercise helped them understand themselves better, and it was a quiet and subtle way to build an internal capacity to own their greatness and fix their challenges.

The key thing is, it wasn't always that way for this community. It used to be one of those communities that didn't understand anything about itself. It didn't know what it had to offer up to the world, and didn't know what challenges were holding it back. Its greatest effort to instigate growth at one time was to put a sign at the edge of town near the highway that read, "Lots for Sale."

My first question to community members at a meeting where I was asked to provide some candid advice was, "Lots of What?" Yes, I know they were selling housing lots. Everyone who drove by knew that too. But whom were they actually selling the lots to? Are there real people driving down long expanses of highway with the sole purpose of finding a bare piece of dirt they could live on? Most people I meet are concerned about the quality of the school, or access to healthcare, or jobs and careers available, or quality of life issues such as parks, recreation, culture, water quality, attractiveness, the types and number of service clubs . . . and an exhaustive list of what makes their community a quality place. To say nothing else about yourself as a community except that you have a vacant piece of dirt for sale isn't advertising anything about your community, except that you may have given up. Success means selling the community, not just selling lots. Failure means having nothing but lots for sale. Lots and lots of lots.

Many communities make the mistake of reaching far beyond the "two-list" exercise without making sure that what they do corresponds with what is valued about the community and connects with what makes it great. They have initial success with the first plan they create, so they get the impression plans are the key to success, and then all the exercises become about plans. They create a business plan, and an economic development plan, and a tourism plan, and a land development plan, and an engagement plan, and a volunteer coordination plan, and then strategy-planning sessions to come up with more plans, and through it all they hire a consultant to write a plan for producing more plans, and of course everyone needs a plan to govern the plans. Soon plan paralysis sets in. All activity becomes focused on making more plans. Plans are important and necessary, but real success comes in carrying out the plans. Success is only achieved through the execution of the plan, not by virtue of simply having a plan. Plans are guideposts, but plans themselves don't act, and don't produce results. Too many plans eliminate action, and eliminating action eliminates success.

Even good plans, when adopted without connecting to what is valued about the community and with what makes it great, can be incredibly counter-productive. There was a wonderful community that had a quality about it that drew people from near and far, though that quality could never be adequately put into script. I will try, however. It was a community of modest size that was about one hour from a larger center. It was not a bedroom community of the city, though. There were bustling but quaint streets with mom and pop stores, full of locals as well as out-of-towners who loved the mystique of the com-munity. There was something about the community that pulled you in and made you feel at home. Few locals ever left town to shop in the big city, and many people from far-off places, sometimes hours away, came to shop and to experience that special indefinable mood produced when you were there. Some described it as a "New England feel." One person said, "It feels like the perfectly quaint, warm, wel-coming community you read about in a Stephen King novel, right before evil shows up, except evil never shows up here. It's just home." Something about it made it great. People felt it and wanted to be a part of that greatness.

Evil did show up, though, in the form of a plan. Somewhere in the process of growing, the community lost sight of *why* they were growing. As I mentioned, the small business community was bustling, families were moving into town, housing prices were strong, the volunteer sector was booming, the school was full, and prosperity was everywhere. The community hired an economic development officer and told her to do whatever economic development offices are supposed to do. So, without further guidance or assistance or communication, the EDO pulled some generic economic development strategies off the Internet to get started. Of course the generic strategies say to attract businesses. The town council put pressure on the EDO to do this quickly, and supported a plan to get the attention of businesses, especially big box stores that were popping up in neighboring communities everywhere. Those box stores came eagerly came to town. They set up between the town and the highway. That changed the look and feel of the community. From the highway it looks now more like a super-mall than a community, and it only took a little more than two years for that to occur. Some around town still refer to the experience as a blitzkrieg, or rather a box-krieg. They will tell you how the box stores came to town in formation and so quickly, like an army of super-enterprises that took over and killed the feel of the community.

With the arrival of those stores the town lost its magic. It lost the quality that had drawn so many to it. People stopped coming to town to shop. Mom and pop stores began closing their doors. Jobs were lost. Housing prices took a fall. People moved away. The community stopped being what it was and became something else that didn't correspond with its values and what made it great. They have since bounced back economically, but they have become the bedroom community of that larger center. Few outsiders come to visit the community anymore because the mojo is gone. That community bought into a plan that didn't support who they were, because at some point they quit thinking about and appreciating their unique identity. They forgot their true value and it cost them their success.

Do not use this story to go to a meeting and say box stores are all bad and should never be let into town, however. That is not what I am saying at all. In this case, box-stores were out of sync with what made the community great. In another case a community welcomed the box stores even when the mom and pop Main Street businesses cried foul and announced their impending doom to everyone. But what they found was the arrival of some big-box stores almost tripled the number of shoppers who came to the community from far and wide. The Main Street shops, with the support of the chamber of commerce and town council, worked hard to draw the same people who came to shop in the box stores down onto Main Street to do shopping there as well. They beautified Main Street, increased the walkability, encouraged open street cafes, and added character and charm. It was great for local commerce. New businesses and restaurants opened and the old ones blossomed anew. They prospered. They all prospered. That wouldn't have happened without the growth in the number of shoppers, which might not have occurred without the advent of the box stores. The point is there is no generic plan that can simply guarantee your success. It takes action, meshed with the values and qualities of your community, which already make it great. Trying to be something you aren't is a sure way to fail.

Sometimes it's not simply about *trying* to be something we really aren't. Sometimes it's about *stumbling* into being something we really aren't. Life is a busy adventure and we are often pulled in so many different directions we spend more time fulfilling obligations than living. The tyranny-of-the-urgent consumes our daily lives and before we know it we don't know where we are, why we are there, or who we are with. It is the root cause of every mid-life crisis. We all have values that direct us to make choices in life, but our values often conflict and we are forced to make choices. With problems and pressure nipping at our heels every day, eventually some values become the default choice while others are compromised and lost in the shuffle . . . for a time. At a middle point in our lives, however, something (often a death) triggers a reflection that causes us to re-evaluate those default choices and we begin to yearn for opportunities to nourish those lost values.

Hollywood would have you believe everyone who goes through a mid-life crisis buys a sports car and tries to fill it with a young blonde, or else they Botox their lips and hire a pool boy, or some combination of those. A few people in a mid-life crisis may do that in an attempt to recapture their youth, but in reality, that just isn't a normal situation. Mid-life crises are more often characterized by a shift of values away from money and stuff to valuing relaxation, or travel, or family, or helping those who have less. We work hard to make enough money so we can afford to travel, but we work so hard we never have enough time to travel until we are too old to actually enjoy the traveling we can now afford to do. We work hard to make enough money to send our kids to the best schools, but then we forget about how much value there is in just spending time with them, watching them grow and building a strong relationship with them. We work hard so we make enough money to donate to worthy causes, but we forget how valuable it is to our souls to volunteer for a not-for-profit that needs people's time and energy, often more than it needs money. And then suddenly one day something happens to wake us up. We realize there has to be more to life than making a living. We re-assess our values and commence the mid-life crisis, where we try to find ourselves again and return to some deep values that have been neglected for too long.

So much could be avoided — mistakes made, opportunities missed, moments that could have been better appreciated — if we simply took the time to assess our values more often. There will still be conflicts in our values, but our challenge these days is not to manage the conflict but to separate what our values *are* from what we perceive our values *should be*. Society says we should always want to work more hours, we should always want to get ahead, we should always want a bigger house, a better car, a bigger TV, and often we buy into those goals without ever stopping to see if we truly value them. It is critical for our own happiness and success that we determine if what we are doing is of real value to us, or if we are simply doing it because the collective mindset has us convinced it is supposed to be a value to us. If we want to be successful we have to be willing to push out some of society's implanted values and reinvigorate our own.

Personal success comes from understanding our values and pursuing them. Success comes to communities that understand what they value, and even more it comes to those who recognize and appreciate those valuable assets they already possess. Until the community does a value assessment and honestly looks at what its true values are, it cannot properly identify what it can become, because it doesn't even know what it is. Sometimes what people *think and say* they value is not necessarily what they truly *do* value. More often, just as with individual people, a community's values are more accurately reflected in its actions than in its words. If a person acts nice to you but is not nice to the waiter, they are not really a nice person. They may say they are nice and show to you they are by treating you nicely, but without realizing it they are demonstrating by their treatment of the waiter they really only value that you think they are a nice person. A community may say it values being small and friendly, but if the actions of the people living there demonstrate they actually don't welcome outsiders, they are deceiving themselves about what they really value. None of that makes the community bad, it just means people are lying to themselves, and the community can't move forward until it faces up to itself. Too often the community will become hostile to anyone who brings forward evidence that contradicts the lie they tell themselves, just as people are prone to do. They will question your motives for saying the community isn't welcoming or is hard to fit into. They will say you are too different and you are the exception rather than the rule. Their lie helps them feel good and helps make their world make sense. You can't challenge that lie without getting attacked, but remember success won't come to those communities that deceive themselves about who they are.

If you are looking to kill your community you have to ignore what is good about it and what could be improved. You have to carry on with the deep-rooted self-deception that allows you to live blind to your own self-created misery and failure. You can't reflect in a way that will lead you to enlightenment because that will force you to change your views and change your actions. You'd do best to hold onto those lies that help you cope with the world and explain away why you fail. Then you will never have to see the truth that it is you who are killing your community.

CHAPTER 5
SHOP ELSEWHERE

I have used the word "community" consistently throughout this book, but I have yet to define exactly what a community is. I should know better since the first rule of debate and philosophy is to define your terms to be certain everyone is talking about the same thing. A community is simply a group of individuals who share an identity based on common interests, common purpose, or shared values. "Community" has a very broad and general meaning. It can refer to a town, but it can also refer to a business, an organization, a professional association . . . in fact the list is almost inexhaustible. I have realized since the first edition of this book, people see these stories as equally applicable to their businesses, as well as their volunteer and professional communities. In fact, that may very well warrant a new book someday. When we consider the development of communities strictly defined as towns, however, we see their origin developed out of a desire to have safety and security.

The focus of this book is not about how communities have formed over the ages so please forgive my very simplified summary of the history of communities. Simply put, the first communities were small bands of people rooted together because they were family. Those families grew into clans still networked and held together by family ties. Those small clans were prone to attacks by roving bandits who would loot, rape and kill as they moved across the countryside. Some small clans became larger clans, and larger clans built protective barriers to defend against the marauders. Inside those protective walls you can imagine the real beginnings of the concept of a community and a society took form. There had to be mechanisms in place to deal with fires, with fights, with food and plans for housing and security and leadership. Those are the places that became towns and cities, and the roots of what we think of as communities.

Those towns grew in size and strength, and in prosperity. Those who stayed in the countryside often remained poorer subsistence farmers still prone to attacks unless they were protected by larger and wealthier landholders. Inside the walls, crafts and trades grew, bartering and trading became commonplace and most importantly, wealth increased. The towns and cities became the hubs of commerce. People shopped their wares and their goods and supplied an ever-increasing range of skilled services and trades to a mass of people not historically assembled together. Thus, the roots of our modern economy grew in large part from a need for mutual protection. Once established, the community would eventually establish a set of shared values. Most modern towns, at least in Europe and North America, had commerce as their core function and chief activity.

A community, in this case a town, achieved success when it had a strong economic foundation at its core. That remains true to this day. That means economic principals, not just an appreciation of shared values or services, must be front and center in any plans to ensure the success of a community. As such, the circulation and growth of money within the community is important to the survival and prosperity of the community itself, since that is fundamental to its foundation. Obviously then, a great way to kill many modern communities is to make sure more money leaves the community than arrives. In essence, you need to see to it that money within the community is spent outside the community. That will result in a reduced level of economic activity, which will eventually weaken and kill your entire community.

Every chamber of commerce in every city or town preaches you should keep your dollars in town and shop locally. We know the importance of this since, according to economists, every dollar spent will touch an average of seven hands within the community before it leaves. That means every one of those dollars has a multiplier effect of seven. That helps your community grow. As well, the more local the business the more impactful the multiplier effect. Local business owners are far more likely to keep the dollars in the community by spending locally, while franchised or corporate businesses will necessarily take a lot of dollars collected in sales and move them out of town to a corporate central office somewhere else. Shopping locally creates jobs and wealth for your community, while every dollar spent outside is in all likelihood gone for good. You really don't need an economist to tell you what a negative effect that can have on a community. That is why chambers of commerce always preach the importance of shopping locally. Shopping elsewhere is a great way to kill your community. So, why do we do it so often?

As much as chambers of commerce preach the message, and as much as we all know the logic behind it, the reason we don't comply with the shopping local maxim is a deep-seated psychological neurosis. I have said it time and again throughout this book, attitude is what determines whether or not our community is going to be successful — and whether we ourselves, for that matter, will be successful along with it. We don't outwardly *choose* to be unsuccessful. There is no conscious choice to fail. Failure is the prodigy of the ill-thought-out and illogical choices we make; choices rooted in wrong attitudes. Wrong attitudes are self-destructive, but we rarely realize the ultimate impact of our attitudes because we don't readily see the immediate consequences of them. The best way to illustrate the point is to relay the three stages in the life of a business in a community.

Stage One happens when a new business first opens. The owners often pour their life savings into the venture with the intent of making some money back over the years, and to grow their community. It may be risky, but it is worth the gamble to the business owner who wants to remain in their community where he or she can make a living and raise a family. What often ensues, however, are seemingly orchestrated negative and nefarious comments from the most evil place on Earth . . . a place where nothing positive is ever said and very little truth is ever spread: the coffee shop. In some places the coffee shop attendees are gently referred to as the "senate," but that would give the impression they are a group of old men with wisdom, when really they are simply miserable people who run everything down. They often do little more than waste time gossiping about and criticizing those in the community who are out actually doing something and too busy to sit around the coffee shop.

So they begin, innocently it seems, to first discuss why anyone would invest their savings to open such a business. The members of the senate support each other about how stupid the idea is, how it will never fly in their town, how no one could possibly make money at that business, how the products will be garbage or too expensive and any other negative word that could be said about the venture. Those will eventually become the excuses to justify why they won't, and don't think anyone else should, patronize that store. The rumors grow out from the coffee shop that the products being sold are junk or a rip-off. People hear that and don't buy from the new store. They don't even go into the store to check it out for themselves. They hear the service is bad, there is no warranty coverage, the business is just about broke, or the business owner is an idiot, or greedy, or lucky, or mean . . . and they don't go shop in that store. The coffee-shop negativity leaks out and dominates the consumer mentality in town, so locals don't spend money in that local store. The essential point of this stage is to ensure people do not patronize the business when it is only in its infancy.

Stage Two occurs if the business survives Stage One, and perhaps even becomes successful. That is when the coffee-shop senate changes its strategy and finds a new front on which to attack. The discussion now focuses on how bad the positives are. Yes, you read right. It focuses on how bad it is the business is doing well. The conversation gets focused on the wealth the business owner and family are acquiring. In the coffee shop, sarcasm drips from envious mouths as they discuss the size of the (new) house, the size of her (new) ring or perhaps his (new) golf clubs, or the make of their (new) car(s). The point of this stage is to stir up jealousy, which will cause more and more local folks to want to not shop in that local business. As a result, consumers drive down the highway to a comparable business in the next community to make their purchases. They deliberately choose to make someone they don't know in a different community wealthier, rather than risk benefitting someone they will have to be jealous of in their own community. They deliberately spend their money out of town, and the dollars they spend are then gone for good.

In the Third Stage the business closes up, and the coffee-shop folk chalk it all up to bad management and brag they were right from the beginning. Sometimes it is because coffee-shop critics were successful in getting the business to go broke, but usually if the business survived Stage One it closes because it was bought out by a larger chain store, or there was simply no one prepared to take it over in the community. Would you want to face those first two stages as a new business owner? Of course not, and after watching the previous business owner go through it, few others want the headache either. That doesn't stop some of those coffee-shop critics from complaining to anyone who will listen: "There is something wrong with the world when we just can't seem to keep a good business in town." That is a direct quote from a fella I met once at a community meeting when a business closed down in his town. He was also identified by his coffee-shop compatriots as the biggest critic of the business all the years it was open. He admitted to me later he never spent a single dollar in that store. He had not realized the consequences resulting from his attitude, or how his attitude had poisoned others toward the business and its owner.

This great work people do in places like the coffee shop to ruin business ventures is all about attitude, but in this case it is all about one prevailing attitude: jealousy. Jealousy is the most evil of all human traits. It is irrational, illogical and destructive because it does not simply harm others but also you and those close to you too. Typically, with jealousy, the more successful your neighbor is, the larger you privately desire their failure to be. When the discussion at the coffee shop is all sneers and jeers about a new business opening, the real reason to run it down is usually not that the business is a poor choice, but rather that there is a deep-seated jealousy or envy toward the person who opened it. As the business succeeds and prospers the real attitude is unveiled and it becomes apparent the negativity is rooted in jealousy over the business owner's success and the "things" success brings.

Jealousy is particularly illogical and irrational when the consequences of jealous wishes are taken to their inevitable conclusion. If you are jealous of the success and wealth your community business owner has and you refuse to shop there because of it and you encourage others not to shop there, in all likelihood the business owner will make less money. If you are lucky, your jealousy will become infectious and many others won't shop there. If you are really lucky, that may cause the business owner to finally go broke and close up shop, and you won't have anything to be jealous of anymore. No more watching them in their new house, or with their new cars, or fretting about their new golf clubs or jewelry. They are gone. Now, don't you feel better? There is nothing to be jealous of because the business owners, their success, and their things are all gone. However, there will still be so many other successful business owners of whom to be jealous. What can be done to end all of your jealousy for good? Fear not! There is hope for more and better consequences that stem from that jealous attitude of yours.

One business owner going broke may not seem like much of a success, but it can have a powerful impact. Not only is there the loss of the business, but there will also be the loss of those jobs in the community. That will mean the economy of your community is smaller, and it may mean the people and families who relied on those jobs have to move away. That means less money flowing in and around your community, and less tax revenue in the community. Less money flowing in the community could cause another business to close its doors; a business and owner probably next in line for your jealousy anyway. That means different families who relied on those jobs are now unemployed, which means even less money flowing in your community, which means the next business you were probably jealous of may close, which means . . . well, you get the picture, I am sure. The effect compounds as the weight of one business closing and the money and jobs lost from it, causes another business to close, and so on.

The same principal applies when it comes to taxes. When a business closes it means the town's expenses have to be spread over a smaller base that includes fewer businesses. Fewer people in town also means the town's expenses have to spread over a smaller population. That means either less gets done in your community, or the taxes go up. Perhaps it means you finally cannot afford the road improvements, or the recreation center repairs, or the new fire truck, or to maintain the playground equipment, or something *you* value. Perhaps it means you opt for really high property taxes, which helps ensure no new people or businesses *can* afford to move to your community. Or perhaps it means you opt for fewer services and a lower quality of life, which helps to guarantee that no new people or businesses *want* to move to your community. Regardless, it works like dominoes and looks like dominoes. One business failure in a small community, thanks to your jealous remarks about town, can put a strain on the others to fail. Each failure leads to new failures.

What starts as simple jealousy and negative talk in the coffee shop, leading so many to spend their money outside of town, becomes a chain reaction of businesses closing and jobs being lost. Eventually your successful campaign will come full circle to hurt you and those close to you. That is why jealousy is so illogical. It is unlikely you, your job, your family, your paved streets, your school, your hospital, your town hall, or much of anything else can survive such an ordeal. Somewhere in that chain reaction of closures and losses your business will be closed or your job will be lost. Embracing jealousy leads to the destruction of the successful person you are jealous of, but that eventually leads to the destruction of your community and your own destruction as well. Being jealous of successful businesses and people in your community is not going to make you successful, but it will absolutely ensure you all share in failure. Jealousy creates a ripple effect across a community that eventually grows to a tsunami-like wave that will sooner or later land on your beach.

You will argue people don't honestly mean others ill when they are jealous and don't cause harm, so I shouldn't be so hard on them. I can hear you saying it. Please recall the central purpose of this book is to point out the very real impact our attitudes have on the success or failure of our communities and ourselves. These are not fanciful tales, but real-life examples, which clearly demonstrate how wrong attitudes destroy communities. Of course we don't see the effects play out immediately or overtly. If we did we might change our behavior like rats being rewarded for pressing the right lever. It is the long-term consequences of decisions stemming from negative attitudes we must avert if we are looking to protect the health of our community. There is no immediate reward or punishment, which means it takes thinking and vision to realize the consequences of our attitudes. Whether it simply means not signing up to volunteer at something because the organizer is so much more popular or smarter than you, or not picking up something you need because you would have to go into "that store" and give "that owner" money, or driving out of town to shop because of that new car the owner parks down the street, the long-term consequences pile up from each little act. It really doesn't matter if it is just a feeling or an attitude, or you think it is just a one-off. It is destructive. Small efforts compound to have great effect, and there is no such thing as a negative attitude or action, no matter how small, that does not have an effect. Of course, if you really want to kill your community, continue with that attitude. You will be just like that high school student who figures there can't possibly be any harm in smoking one little joint.

Allowing your jealousy to destroy businesses without realizing the impact it will have on you is not something that just happens inside communities. It is something that happens between communities as well. It has been quite a while since I ran for my first nomination for the Legislative Assembly, but I clearly remember a discussion I had with an accountant at a vehicle- repair shop in a county that neighbored mine. I was anxious to present my case for why she should support my efforts to win the nomination of the party. I had worked hard to prepare, so as I won her over with my ideas my confidence grew. At the end, she paused as if to size me up and asked me one question I had not prepared for at all. She asked me how she could be sure, if elected, I wouldn't go to the capitol and simply fight for my county and leave theirs to fail.

That was a great question. I had neglected to consider the rivalry existing between the two municipal districts for longer than I had been alive. Each district had fought the other's success for generations, somehow thinking if the other was weaker they would grow stronger. She was concerned I would follow the historic trend and fight the success in her district, hoping it would make my district stronger. My response must have been persuasive, because not only did she agree to support my candidacy, she became an active campaigner on our behalf. My answer to her was simple: "It is not possible for one area of the constituency to be prosperous and successful while other parts do poorly. We rise together or die together." It is not possible for you to be successful while everyone you are jealous of in your community fails. Likewise, it is also not likely you will be successful if all your neighboring communities are failing. If one grows, the others have the opportunity to do well too. If one does poorly the others can eventually be dragged down. Simply put, no one region can truly prosper in isolation. There is no such thing as a win-lose relationship in cases like this. We all win or we all lose.

It is important chambers of commerce are actively teaching and preaching about the benefits of shopping locally. It is unfortunate no chamber, to my knowledge, teaches or preaches to its own membership about the importance of giving members of the community a *reason* to shop locally. Whenever we spend money, we usually like to feel we got the best bang for our buck and our dollar was well earned by the business we patronized. Some examples were given in Chapter 2, "Don't Attract Business," about the importance of price, quality, selection and service when it comes to attracting people to spend money in your store. It is unfortunate some business owners have so strongly bought in to the belief you must shop locally they have all but abandoned the competitive values that would encourage them to earn your dollar. Instead it seems they expect you to shop in their stores as though it is some sort of moral imperative that requires no matching effort or focus from them.

Have you ever entered a business and noticed customer service was dependent upon the business owner's mood? Perhaps you have noticed the quality of the work you get is conditional on whether your son or his son won the hockey game last night? Perhaps you get an unwelcome look and a price increase if you come into the store at the wrong time. Regardless of the reason, it is disheartening and discouraging to a customer to experience that. I understand businesses have the right to go out of business by offering poor price, quality, selection and service. That is the nature of the free market. Business owners do not, however, have the right to complain when they are the very reason the customers are leaving . . . yet so many of them do just that.

Recall the story from Chapter 2 about the mayor who owned a gas station and managed to chase away everyone who tried to open up competing stations. He charged a lot more for his gasoline than neighboring communities because there was no competition in his own town. The result was that many people from the community filled up elsewhere whenever they were out of town to avoid paying the "mayor's gas tax." I was the guest speaker at that town's chamber meeting when that former mayor/current gas station owner actually complained publicly how fewer and fewer people seemed to realize the need to shop locally because they were always heading out of town to shop. The other business owners and I were completely lost for words until one of them finally challenged him that his really high prices were causing people to leave town, and that it was impacting all the other businesses in town too. As quite frequently happens, when people leave town to get gas they also for lunch, stop at the hardware store for supplies, and get groceries in the other town while there. In other words, it was not only money the former mayor could have earned that was leaving town, but money other businesses could have earned was leaving as well. Still, even after it was made clear through irrefutable evidence about the impact of his pricing, the gas station owner insisted people had an obligation to shop locally. He expected them to pay an exorbitantly higher price. He believed he didn't have to give them a reason to shop locally. He kept his price the same, money continued to leave town, and he continue to complain consumers didn't understand the impact of spending their money out of town. He denied any ability to change habits or to take responsibility for it.

The relationship between the customer and the shop owner is a little bit like a marriage, or at least it should be. In a marriage, if either or both partners take the other for granted it is not long before they start to feel unappreciated and unloved, and that is when the marriage falls apart. There was a resident of one community I worked with who prided himself on being a community booster and who was apparently regarded as very dedicated to his community. Let's call him Bruce. As it turned out, Bruce was the epitome of a man who took his local businesses for granted. Bruce would hit up everyone to donate for any and all of the groups, committees and functions for which he volunteered. He was a relentless and active volunteer in his community, so businesses would donate. Actually, Bruce was one of the best fundraisers in the community . . . at least for a while. Eventually the donations began to dry up, especially when Bruce asked for them. The reason was that Bruce did all of his business dealings in other communities. No one seemed to know why. I am sure Bruce had his reasons, but he didn't see the irony in asking for donations for community causes from businesses in his community that he didn't support. The business owners saw it and simply stopped donating.

Business owners can help in a variety of ways to keep the romance alive. Cleaning or perhaps beautifying your business once in a while keeps up the appeal. Helping customers with their bags to their vehicles on occasion can be a pleasant surprise. Opening the door for them, asking how their families are doing, or occasionally just a warm smile is all it takes to lift a customer's spirits and make them feel they are valued. It works for strangers so why wouldn't it work for customers you want to keep coming back to your store? Sometimes that is all it takes to make them want to come back. Both the business owners and members of the community have to remember not to take each other for granted. I don't want to over-emphasize the marriage comparison, but it is important to show appreciation and understanding. It helps you grow together instead of growing apart.

If you want to be certain to kill your community, it is incredibly important you take each other for granted. You may want to invest time building a culture of jealousy around the community by spreading falsehoods and negativity at your local coffee shop. This will encourage dollars to leave town and your local economy to shrink, which will make the entire community poorer and poorer. If you are determined enough, your entire town, its businesses and its people will go financially, morally and spiritually bankrupt. Then and only then can you let the last of your jealousy go, because there will be no one and nothing of which to be jealous.

CHAPTER 6
DON'T PAINT

Yes, you read the chapter title correctly. If you want to ensure your community fails then don't paint. Of course greater failure will come to your community if you include other de-beautification plans to the list. Don't dust, or sweep, or wash windows, or mow grass, or pick up garbage, or plant flowers, or anything else of the sort. Essentially, if you want to kill your community, then do not do anything that will make it look visually appealing. It's just that simple.

I am sure you have a slightly twisted look on your face as you contemplate the superficiality of the preceding paragraph. After all, what I have just suggested is we can actually judge a book by its cover, which goes against all that we were taught as children. We were told not to make this mistake because what the cover shows is not necessarily indicative of the contents. We are supposed to look at what people are like on the inside, beyond their physical appearance; like their depth of character and integrity. That is sound and valuable advice. I believe there is a common phrase about putting lipstick on a pig that summarizes why that is important, so I won't delve into it any further.

What is also true is people often do judge books by their covers. Ugly books simply don't get picked up and read. Publishers design covers that will lure readers into picking up that book and giving it a browse. The covers may be bright and colorful, may be hardcover or leathery, may have provocative titles, or they may simply present a provocative image to attract a potential reader. Regardless, publishers know they need to put an interesting cover on a book to get a reader to pick it up, or they simply would not spend so much time and expense designing them as they do. The first edition of this book had captivating and poignant cover art, designed by the very talented Rick Sealock, which garnered a few American awards — the very fact you're reading this sentence might suggest the second edition's cover, also designed by Rick, is at least as effective. The title of this book is also meant to be enticing and provocative. When I gave my very first presentation on this subject matter I wanted to challenge people to think differently. I could have titled the presentation and this book *How Right Attitudes Can Build a Strong Community*, but I don't know anyone who would have come to listen, or picked up the book to read. It would have been too boring and lecture-like, which everyone who has heard me attests is not the case. Ugly-covered books may have amazing content inside, but if no one picks them up and no one reads them, their value isn't appreciated, which means their value is lost.

First impressions are truly the beginning of everything. "Thin-slicing" is a term first used in 1992 by psychologists, Nalini Ambady and Robert Rosenthal. It is used to describe the ability and the value of forming judgments based on very little information at the moment of that first impression. A judgment gleaned from the small amount of first-impression data acquired by the mind can often prove to be more accurate then later assessments made with more information. It's a case for trusting your gut instincts, which are simply feelings or judgments your brain presents to you based on information you have not had time to become conscious of. That doesn't mean you should always trust your gut instincts, or that all truth lies in those first impressions. What it does mean is you need to be consciously aware of the first impression you make on other people, and that perhaps you should consider the impact the first impression of your community makes on outsiders.

If I had the power of Zeus I would love to do an experiment where I pluck a nice family in a minivan off a street in Detroit (no offence to Detroit) and plunk them softly down on any street in your community. What would they do? How would they react? I have been in a lot of communities where I am confident the family would roll up the windows, lock the doors and drive like hell to get out of there. Their experiences say neighborhoods like that, streets that look like those, aren't safe places. To you, your community may be a great place, and you may know it to be very safe, but how would others view the streets in your community? I can already hear some of you saying in your minds, "Who cares what that family would think? We aren't trying to attract families from Detroit." OK, fair enough, but you wouldn't be reading this book if you weren't concerned for your community's future. You should already know your success depends on attracting more people. So who are you trying to attract, and how will they see your community? The impression your community presents is important.

Your community may seem fine to you. You may know it is safe. You may know it is a great place to live. But will people who drive or walk through it get that impression? You can lament how unfair it may be for newcomers to form such a quick judgment, but those lamentations are wasted energy, because they won't make your situation better. Imagine the first few minutes and the first impression of your community are like a job interview. Did you show up at the interview neat and presentable? Did you dress for the job you want, or the job you have? Did you look and sound confident and successful? Was your hair done? Were your teeth brushed? If you show up at the interview unkempt and slovenly, you may be the smartest person in the world, and perfect for the job, but the impression you give the interviewer doesn't say that and you probably won't get the job. Lament all you want about not getting the job, it won't make the outcome any better. You should have cleaned yourself up and given an impression that matches what you know is on the inside. The same applies to your community.

I was talking through some of these concepts with my wife and she suddenly insisted on taking me shopping. Normally I hate shopping, but in the face of her insistence I let her take me to two large and popular department stores. At the time I was not aware both department store chains were actually owned by the same parent company. I also learned from the shopping experience about half of the goods in each store were the same, although those goods were sold at very different prices. The first store she took me to had linoleum flooring, and many of the linoleum pieces were curling up in places or had come completely off, leaving only the tracts of dried glue to walk on. The stock on the shelves wasn't stacked neatly, and in some places it looked as though a hurricane had blown through. The staff seemed to want to be anywhere but at work, appeared irritated, and sloughed around in badly fitting and worn-out department store uniforms. I noted the prices on some particular items, which my wife assured me were excellent deals. There was an odor in the store I didn't really notice until we left, and then I couldn't shake it loose. It lingered in my mind for hours after.

Later that day we went to the second store. It was noticeably fancier than the first store. Walking in, I noticed beautiful clean carpets resembling runways between garment racks that were all neatly and orderly hung and easy to access. Everything smelled good, the place looked good, and soothing music played in the background. We weren't there two minutes before a kind and grandmotherly woman approached us and asked if we needed help finding anything. My wife showed me the same products as I had identified and priced in the other store and to my astonishment the prices on those identical products were remarkably higher than at the previous location. I presumed the fancier store would have trouble moving that portion of its merchandise that could be bought for less in its sister store. I was wrong. The fancier store was more financially stable and profitable, and in fact, the first store closed its doors a few years after my wife took me on that tour. It still didn't make sense to me at first. Why would anyone go to the fancier store to pay twice as much for the same goods they could buy in the other store? My wife reminded me of my own points about first impressions and esthetics. General social affluence enables people to choose a pleasant shopping experience over simply shopping for value. People will choose to shop in a place that is friendly and inviting, and yes, aesthetically pleasing when they have the option and ability.

We all want to be surrounded by aesthetically pleasing things. We want to be with beautiful people in beautiful places. We want to wear beautiful clothes and drive beautiful cars back and forth from our beautiful homes to our beautiful work, stopping on occasion to hang with our beautiful friends in beautiful restaurants or lounges for beautiful meals on beautiful days. We are naturally drawn to and inspired by beauty. Not one person on earth has ever looked across a crowded room, seen a person they thought was ugly, and proceeded to cross the room and ask him or her out. Do you know anyone (hipsters excluded) who has ever walked into a car dealership and asked to see all the ugly cars? No one meets with a real estate agent to purchase a house and insists "ugly" be one of the distinguishing features of the home. We all want to be surrounded by beautiful places and people. We are all attracted to aesthetically pleasing things.

My wife and I went looking for a house shortly after we were married. As we cruised through listings and living rooms I noted there were specific houses my wife liked and others she really didn't, but I couldn't really determine what attributes of the different houses were driving her opinions. I finally got it when our realtor said, "Sue, you are going to love this house. It has great curb appeal." It's a common realtor term I had not heard before, but suddenly it all made sense to me. If the impression from the curb was that the lawn was nicely manicured and looked well taken care of and flowers were planted in the flowerbeds and such, then my wife was initially impressed with the house. It looked like it could be a home, our home, and she suddenly opened up to the options and opportunities the house presented. However, if the house lacked curb appeal when we pulled up because it was run down and unkempt, it often didn't matter as much what the house looked like on the inside, because she had already been turned off. Real estate agents know how impactful curb appeal is in selling a house and often advise their clients on how to improve curb appeal.

When invited to help a community identify how to turn itself around I usually make the first order of business a walk from one end to the other. Driving is a valuable way to do a quick assessment of what your community looks like, but it doesn't give you the right impression about what it *feels* like. Those are two very different things and the latter is where curb appeal takes shape. Most people form a weak impression of a house when they pull up in a vehicle. The strong curb appeal impression comes when they first set foot on the sidewalk in front of a house. That impression is formed when all of the senses take hold. It is at that moment you can see the house most clearly. It is at that moment when you can smell the grass and trees and flowers, or the lack of them. It is at that moment you hear the kids playing next door or a dog barking down the street. It is at that moment the home changes from being a picture to a being part of a neighborhood. Walking around your town, rather than driving, will give you a cleaner and richer sense of its curb appeal. Walking around town will help you get a better sense of who your community is and will help you see what needs to be fixed. Walking around will give you a better sense of and a keener appreciation of your community's aesthetic, or lack thereof.

Frankly, some of you reading this may still be skeptical about the importance of aesthetics and think I am still placing too much emphasis on beauty. In fact, most communities I have visited, even when they appreciate the value of aesthetics in their quest for growth, still put it on their list of things to do as a "nice-to-have" that will be done after all of the important things are taken care of. Being aesthetically pleasing, however, is not just a nice-to-have. It can't wait until everything else is done. We aren't simply attracted to aesthetically pleasing things, we actually judge things by their aesthetic value, and it is not just a superficial quality. We are genetically bred to be attracted to aesthetically pleasing things. That's right. It is part of our subconscious thought processes and inseparable from our existence. Our genetic makeup leads us to beauty.

All animals are attracted to beauty as part of a built-in self-preserving instinct. Imagine a female cheetah walking through the jungle, and suddenly it hits her that it is time to start looking for a mate. She comes to a clearing where she sees two male cheetahs. She looks them over, notes one of them has bright eyes, nice clean shiny fur, sharp claws and teeth, and strong shoulders. He looks attractive and healthy and strong. The other cheetah has a broken tail, mangy fur, droopy ears, an infected eye and looks like it hasn't eaten in days. He looks unhealthy, sickly and weak. Which do you think she is attracted to? Which do you think she will choose as a mate? She isn't just looking for strong muscles or a handsome face or hoping for a jaguar. She is looking for a good mate, and those aesthetically-pleasing attributes are the most telling outward signs of whether that cheetah will be a good provider. It is not merely superficial. It is very real.

So it is with communities. Those aesthetic aspects of a community are the outward signs of what lies way down deep. A beautiful appearance is a telling sign about whether a community has confidence and pride in itself. If a community invests in its parks and its flowers, in its sidewalks and Main Street, in its entrance sign and its street signs, it has shown a desire to invest in itself. It has shown it believes it is successful, its future is bright and it is worth investing in. That doesn't mean the investments I am referring to must all come from the town budget. Most often this is not the case, but in situations where it is, the investment often turns out to be superficial and short-lived. In successful communities the investment in beautification is supported by local government, but investment also comes from businesses, from homeowners, from volunteer groups and from industry — in other words, the initiatives are owned by everyone. Such initiatives show an investment in the entire community by the entire community. That takes the investment from superficial and shallow to something deep and a reflection of meaningful values. It demonstrates a real confidence in the community and a real investment by its members in each other.

Communities have found many ways to improve their curb appeal and enhance that first impression. Some have taken the title of this chapter literally and turned matters around just by utilizing paint. Others have painted their fire hydrants to brighten up the corners of town, or hired professional artists to paint historic murals on large bare walls that would otherwise be unattractive. One community went so far as to arrange a regular event they called "paint week." Everyone brought all their older and partial cans of paint to a central location where someone with aesthetic savvy would mix and blend paints with the help of a paint-recycling expert into fantastic, bright color schemes. Everyone would then gather on a following weekend to paint some pre-identified old fences, old buildings and other deteriorating fixtures that were bringing down the aesthetic value of the community. Most buildings had been abandoned, but some were coordinated with property owners who wanted to do something to help the community improve its aesthetic, but didn't know what to do themselves. There was a significant recognition in all of these communities that paint was a simple way to improve the community they lived in. They recognized that beautification had an inherent value that enhanced the quality of life of the residents, increased their curb appeal and improved the community's prospects for future success.

Other communities have found other ways to improve their curb appeal. Granted, some of them are more expensive than simply painting, but more and more jurisdictions are creating programs accessible to communities that are intended to improve their aesthetics. Main Street improvement programs operate differently in different localities, but their existence is a great opportunity for a community to instigate change. Some of the programs focus on restoring the old fronts to original buildings to add an element of heritage, nostalgia and character to Main Streets, while others adopt a theme for downtown improvements. Others have focused on improving the walkability of downtown cores with wider sidewalks that can accommodate open-air cafes and street shopping. Still others have filled vacant lots on Main Street with small parks all done by volunteers and local business owners who wanted a warmer feel in the core. Regardless, all of those initiatives were intended to improve the feel of the community by improving its aesthetic value, and it worked.

There are a lot of communities trying to find answers and resources to meet the new challenge of creating an aesthetic appeal. I have talked to many town councils that asked me for ideas to complement what they had already put in place to beautify their communities. I always find it ironic many of the communities that recognize the intrinsic value of good aesthetics adhere to a local system of taxation that completely discourages private residents or businesses from sprucing up their own private property. Often when a resident or a small business tries to make improvements, even by the simple environmentally friendly act of planting a few trees, the taxes on that property go up. It is self-defeating for a local government to work on policies to encourage investment in beautification and property enhancements when those investments directly lead to an increase in taxes. Every community that recognizes and appreciates the value of beautification should work to ensure their taxing structure does not work counter to their policies. In fact, every local government should work to see their taxing structure does not run counter to any of their policies' implementation — otherwise, those policies might just as well be disregarded. Taxation is supposed to be a tool for policy implementation, not the other way around.

I worked with one community that developed tax incentives and reductions for businesses that invested to beautify their Main Street business assets. The program was a smashing success, as almost every business took advantage of the offer. They painted their stores, they rebuilt their storefronts, and put planters and benches along the sidewalks in front. Two old abandoned buildings on Main Street were purchased by a local business co-op, renovated and painted, and sold to new business owners under the program. They made Main Street attractive again. The result was heavy traffic throughout that first summer. People from far-off towns came to see the transformation and they spent money in the local businesses. The town administrator confirmed it was hard to get the program started. The town would have to forgo tax revenue for a few years and that wasn't a very popular plan, until one councilor pointed out what they would lose in tax revenue if Main Street businesses continued to close up. The tax revenue lost through the program was more than made up for by the businesses that stayed open for years after and the two new businesses that were now open. The town is now considering options for a similar program for residential properties to encourage homeowners to beautify their properties.

There are numerous excellent groups that communities can turn to for advice in implementing these programs. Communities in Bloom, for example, is an organization that operates around the world encouraging efforts to beautify communities with flowers. They help provide wonderful information to community volunteers, run competitions that reward the efforts and effects of those volunteers, and provide recognition to the achievements of communities that participate in the program. The purpose is not just to clean up garbage and plant flowers around the town, but to also leave a lasting appreciation for, and encouragement to, the people of participating communities to take pride in what they have. The work of volunteers within communities is infectious. Homeowners and businesses often dive into the mix, planting beautiful gardens and flower arrangements in their back and front yards, and making sure that flowers are seen everywhere around town. People who haven't tidied up their yards in years begin planting flowers and painting fences as they jump on the beautification bandwagon. Few want to be left behind when success is in the air, or to have their property stand out as ugly when beauty takes hold. People love to be near beautiful things. We all do.

I've seen many towns and villages, using just a little elbow grease, make their dumpy, dusty, run-down-looking communities appear successful and vibrant. I must emphasize they made their run-down-looking communities *look* successful and vibrant, because in all honesty, they were really just changing the surface appearance of their community. There is always the chance a community that looks beautiful on the surface may not be all that pretty deep down inside. However, I have seen many communities that worked on improving their first impression with investments in aesthetics, only to discover it led to real changes in their attitudes and their belief in their ability to succeed. It may sound like an over-simplification, but think about how you feel about yourself after you buy a sharp new suit, or after you get your hair done. It is really only a superficial change, but it improves your confidence and sense of self-worth. Feeling better about who you are can lead to real improvements in who you are in actuality. As the saying goes, "Beauty may only be skin deep, but ugly goes right to the bone."

I am a firm believer that what we project to others about ourselves becomes reality. If you aren't a kind person, but you want others to believe you are and so you hold doors open for people and act kind, you may become a kind person for real. If you want to become a strong person others rely on and you act that way, you will become a strong person others rely on. Choose who you want to be, act that way for long enough, and you will become that person because you will form habits that make you that person. The same applies for communities. If you want to be a confident and successful community with a future that attracts others, then project those qualities in everything you do. Act like you mean it, learn what you need to do to support those actions, and guess what? You will become that community in real life.

However, if you want to achieve failure, you must look like you are failing. Don't paint. Of course, that is only a superficial form of failure. Really looking like a failure may take a concerted effort to turn your town ugly. Of course, that will only create the facade of failure, it will only create the illusion your town is dying, and in essence it will only put an ugly cover on your book. With patience, however, no one will pick up that book to read and no one will be attracted to your community, and eventually that illusion of failure will become your reality.

CHAPTER 7
DON'T COOPERATE

From our first day in kindergarten we have all been taught the importance of learning how to cooperate with each other. Some of us learn the lesson sooner and better than others. Some don't learn the lesson at all, but even if we fail to put into practice what we learn, we still understand the importance of the lesson. Almost everything takes cooperation to be successful. It doesn't matter if it is in your business, your marriage, or your sports team, cooperation is required. Unless you just arrived on the planet and have never seen another human being in your life, you have had some point or moment when you have cooperated with others and have experienced the value that comes with cooperating. Some of you may even have experienced cooperation on such a high level you discovered synergy, which is the effect of accomplishing a higher quality and quantity of work because you act as a group rather than a collection of individuals. Regardless, if you want to ensure the death of your community, you must not cooperate with other people, with other organizations, or with other communities.

The volunteer base for taking action to build your community is often limited in capacity, which means an effective strategy for failure is to see that your volunteers refuse to work or cooperate with one another in growing your community. You can refuse to cooperate on an individual level, or you can expand that to refusing to allow your group or service club to partner with another group or service club on a shared project of interest. Better still, try your hardest to prevent your entire community from partnering with neighboring communities, especially when those other communities understand how working together assures everyone a greater chance of success than working independently. That will guarantee volunteers get burnt out, frustrated and alienated, never experience synergy and never experience success. It is one surefire way to ensure failure.

The choice to not cooperate is merely a passive method to make certain the failure of your community, and as a result can lack true effectiveness. Refusing to work with another person on a project will simply mean that person and others will proceed with a project without you. You may feel the project is doomed to failure without your expertise, brilliance and magnetic personality, but in reality few of us are as important and critical to a multi-person enterprise as we'd like to believe. Personally, I rarely take a day off for fear everyone I work with will suddenly realize they can function quite well without me. Joking aside, those you refuse to work with will proceed down their paths regardless of your presence, will probably cooperate with each other, and in all likelihood will succeed.

If you want to be certain those volunteers do not proceed with projects without you, you must work to become what I term a Lone Hyena Leader. This type of leader should not be viewed as the alpha of a pack of wolves, but rather a hyena in a pack of scraggly and weak house dogs . . . and they like it that way. They aren't heroes and they aren't brave. They surround themselves with weak and vulnerable people, who go along with whatever the lone hyena says or does because they are usually happy to be on the lone hyena's good side, lest they be lunch. The Lone Hyena Leader keeps everything bundled up and hidden from the rest of the group so he or she alone holds the knowledge of what is happening. If the Lone Hyena is sick, no one knows what to do. If he has a family emergency, everything stops. If he decides to move in another direction, not only is he the only one who knows why, but most of the rest of the group don't even know it hap-pened until it is too late to do anything but go along. The Lone Hyena Leader keeps control that way, and keeps others from venturing off to get work done or form strategic partnerships with other groups or other communities. It is a very successful and commonly seen strategy for failure of an organization.

The Lone Hyena Leader is a model of poor leadership style, but so is someone I like to call Road Block Roger. Roger gets his power strictly from a position of authority with a role as an elected councilor, administrator, manager or chair of some board or committee. He has the same modus operandi as the Lone Hyena Leader. He wants to be the one in charge and much like the Lone Hyena Leader he doesn't know what it means to lead or be a real leader. Both share another characteristic: neither knows what to do with the authority he has acquired. They both know they want to keep that authority, however, and the only way they know how to do that is flex it when they can. What do you do when you don't know how to lead, you don't have any real leadership skills, and you don't understand what is going on, but you want to show you have control and are determined to keep control? You say "No," to demonstrate your authority. Road Block Roger exercises his authority by saying no a lot, particularly to anything he doesn't understand — which is just about everything. He fears being shown up or made irrelevant by allowing someone else to take control of a situation or to become the lead on a project or over an issue. Solutions and ideas get brought forward, but he shows off his power and keeps control by saying no. He likes throwing up road-blocks as a symbol of his authority and he uses this technique as often as he can because he often has very little, if anything else, to offer.

Real leaders understand it takes a team to be successful and that they as leaders are replaceable. In fact, real leaders strive to be replaceable because they see the organization or the goal as larger than themselves. Real leaders also know their role is to find ways to say, "Yes" to their team, and spend most of their own energy on helping each member of the team be successful. That is what success looks like in a healthy organization with a real leader. I know there are a lot of consultants telling people, communities, businesses and organizations success is not a sprint. They are correct. It is not a sprint. They tell everyone now, success is a marathon. That metaphor is meant to suggest success doesn't come quickly or overnight, but rather takes endurance and perseverance to achieve. Although that is true, they are wrong to use that metaphor. It gives the impression that achieving success is an endurance race, but such a race is run from start to finish by the same person. The successful leader knows that is not true. It takes a team to generate enduring success. The "one person theory" is exactly what the Lone Hyena Leader and Road Block Roger want everyone to believe. They want the final say on everything so no one can venture off. They keep control that way. They feel important that way. They feel like leaders that way. They aren't.

The better metaphor for a picture of success for any community or organization is a baton race that never ends. Each runner carries the baton for his or her leg of the race, running at the fastest pace they can manage. At the end of their leg, they pass the baton on to someone else who is conditioned and primed for his or her leg, ready to take the baton and run at their fastest pace, knowing at the end of their leg they will pass it on to someone else, and so on forever. Thinking of it in those terms means your organization must have vigorous succession planning in place. It means you must know your time as a leader is limited and it is your responsibility to not only help train and encourage the next runner or an entire team of runners, but to smoothly hand over the baton to the next one when your time is done. It means recognizing the success of your community, your organization, the project or the business is not all about you. It is about the team you build. Real leaders actively plan for their own demise through succession planning because they view the cause as larger than themselves. Lone Hyena Leaders and Road Block Rogers want admiration and power, so they never support collaboration.

However, even if your entire group refuses to work with other groups, or your community as a whole rejects the invitation to work with neighboring communities, there is always a chance you will still not cause the collective failure of those others. The reality is those other groups or communities beyond the reach of the Lone Hyena and Road Block Roger will carry on and may even achieve success. You may suggest that regardless of the other groups' or communities' efforts you can still cause the failure of your own group or community, but understand you, your group and your community are not islands unto themselves. No matter how much you wish to fail, the success of the groups and communities you refuse to cooperate with could still spill over into your community and consequently, regardless of your own passive refusal to cooperate, you may experience a trickle-down of success.

Fear not, though — there is another, more effective way, to ensure the failure of your group or community. Rather than taking the *passive* approach of simply refusing to cooperate with others, you can take an *active* approach and begin an aggressive campaign to compete with those other groups within your community, or even with other neighboring communities, if the opportunity presents itself. Competing ensures groups and communities are directly pitted against each other even when they have the same goals, thereby expending precious resources on the battle rather than on the goal. This method is very simple to follow through on, and it can ensure not only your group and community fail but also that failure extends to neighboring groups and communities. This will safely inoculate your community from the unwanted success of your neighbors, and will make it certain that your campaign to bring about its own failure is fully effective.

In one community I worked with there were three community organizations that had all decided they needed a new community hall. Residents had discussed for some time the need for such a hall and were prepared to support the building of one. So, all three groups set to work. Oh, I should clarify that in this community of 2000 people, the three organizations were each vigorously working to build their own separate community halls. This in itself may seem ridiculous, but it gets worse. They had all independently decided they did not want to be passive participants in killing their community simply by refusing to cooperate in the construction of one hall. They decided to be active participants in the community's demise, so each group competed for the same volunteer base, the same community fundraising dollars, the same government grants, and even the same lot in town for the building site. Of course, few people wanted to contribute to three separate community halls, so they refused to donate their time and energy, or their money. Understandably, the town wouldn't give the building lot to any of the groups because they did not want to be seen as choosing a winner in the competition. The government, faced with three competing grant requests for identical projects in the same community, refused all of them. Two of the groups even decided to have fundraising dinners on the same night in a bid to outdo the other in the fight for the community hall. No one in the community showed up to either dinner. One of the organizations went broke and the second was close to it.

Those three organizations did everything they could to actively compete with each other, and successfully ensured no community hall was built for almost ten full years. The organizations that barely survived the competing fundraising dinner debacle had little left in the way of money or volunteers to continue the fight. They finally saw the light and began to cooperate with the last remaining organization. Within two years of an agreement to work together they had raised most of the money they needed, had a strong volunteer base and had completed construction of the hall. They accomplished in two years of cooperation what almost a decade of competition had managed to prevent: success.

Competition is not just a valuable tool for bringing about failure in one community. Competition between communities is an excellent way to ensure an entire region fails. Amazingly enough, only a short distance from the community I spoke of in the preceding paragraph was another community that seemed equally determined to bring about its own failure. The two communities were in very close proximity, but they refused to cooperate. Together they were able to bring about failure for the entire region. In fact, they had managed to compete for anything and everything, to the detriment of both, decade after decade after decade. Never had their ability to extend their competition to the point of mutual failure been clearer than when an industrial corporation came to the communities to see about building a new manufacturing plant in the area. The corporation had expressed interest because of the available labor force, the proximity to the rail shipping lines, and the lower cost of business there. They expressly asked the two neighboring communities to jointly work on how they would address the increased need in housing, the growth in the school population and demand for health services, how they would share tax revenue, as well as manage any other growth pressures that would result from a new manufacturing plant. The corporation knew one community could not handle all of the growth caused by the project so they wanted cooperation. These were concerns many municipalities across North America would love to have.

Unfortunately, the communities did exactly what they needed to do to guarantee collective failure. Instead of working together they competed and argued over who would get what share of revenue. They argued about where the plant would be located, where the people would live, where the children would go to school, which hospital should be expanded, and who should get more of the revenue generated. They had the responsibility to come up with collective solutions to handle growth pressures, but not the right to decide where people got to live, or where employees' kids would go to school. Yet, that is what they focused on because they knew it would keep them divided. They spent all of their energy trying to grab what they could from the other, hoping all the success derived from the manufacturing plant would not benefit the other community. They did not cooperate as the corporation had hoped they would. They did more than simply not cooperate, however. They actually ran each other down to the CEO of the corporation through nasty letters they wrote to her. They even began to argue and run each other down in a face-to-face meeting with her, and then told me how unprofessional she was when she finally gave up and walked out of that meeting when they wouldn't quit arguing.

The competition was so vehement and so successful each community managed to chase away the project from the other. If they had both exhibited a passive refusal to cooperate with one another it might have meant one community would have received the project anyway. In that case success would have spilled over into the neighboring community and eventually they might have realized they could work together and both could benefit. Indeed, if they had started off cooperating they might have landed that construction plant and perhaps other business projects in the future, thereby solidifying long-term economic success for them both. Instead, active competition meant both communities got to enjoy the sweet smell of failure — both their own and their neighbor's. Their dedication to competing in such a fashion created the combined failure of the region, and thanks to the reputation they now have, it has promised failure for many years to come because no one wants to do business with either of them anymore.

The current challenge most communities have is in how they define what, or rather who, is in their community. It seems most of the work we do with communities now is in helping them to get beyond the "lines in the sand" drawn 100 to 250 years ago, depending on where you are in North America. Far too many communities focus on municipal lines that were drawn so long ago, and they hold a reverence for them as though those made up lines are all that separate good from evil. Those lines were drawn back when we had to walk everywhere, or if we were lucky, we got to ride a horse. That's it. Often those lines were drawn based on how far kids could walk to school. The economy was based on how far you could haul your produce to a central market by foot or by cart. Politics was based on how far the local newspaper could be delivered in a morning. Everything was local. Everything. So boundaries were drawn based on managing those local areas.

The world has changed. Now we have high speed internet, flights that can take you around the world as fast as it takes you to walk to town, and a global economy that sees products bought online from anywhere in the world arriving at your door in a matter of days, if not a few hours. The boundaries were drawn to reflect a world that doesn't exist anymore. Yet, so many of our leaders and community members hold onto those boundaries. They hold onto those lines drawn in the sand, by someone who couldn't possibly have comprehended what the world would be like today. They use those lines to protect little fiefdoms of power and they use them to keep us divided. Honestly, we aren't competing with each other anymore. We are competing against the rest of the world and if we don't learn to work together we will all fail. Those lines were never meant to keep us apart, and those who use them today to do just that will secure their failure . . . and yours.

I must clarify there is a distinction to be made between the competition I so openly embraced and discussed in Chapters 2 and 5 and the competition I am rather critical of in the preceding paragraphs. In all cases the competition is vigorous, but in the earlier chapters the competition is for the betterment of the community as a whole, while the type of competition I have discussed in this chapter benefits no one and invariably brings about failure. There are clearly times when competition is healthy and times when cooperation is the best method for success. Competition in individual sports such as boxing or golf is the only way those sports work, since a cooperative approach would drastically reduce ticket sales and viewership. Parents are successful when they cooperate in raising children, but it would not be successful if parenting were based on competition. Success comes in knowing when to use cooperation and competition, and the judgment should center around whether or not it is bettering your community.

I have discussed how passively refusing to cooperate can assist in killing your community, and how actively competing against other groups or communities can complete the job to perfection. Passively refusing to cooperate means others will simply carry on with their business as usual and should they have success it will likely spill over into your group or community whether you want it to or not. Actively engaging in competition can ensure you and other communities and groups expend valuable resources in fighting each other, which can help arrange their reduced success, which in turn can aid in your desire to fail. In that case, other communities or organizations may simply choose to avoid your community or organization altogether, which weakens your chance to secure failure.

If passive and active non-cooperation are not effective enough for you and you want to be absolutely assured of failure for yourself and others, there is still another technique you can harness in your campaign to kill your community. Initially I didn't believe the stories I had heard about this maleficent force, even though the testimony was compelling, until I personally bore witness to it. Since then I have listened closely and sought out other stories. I have realized my initial impression that such a mythical beast couldn't exist was wrong, but wrong too was my anticipation that such a creature must be the rarest of all life forms. I have heard testimony from community after community confirming not only that the creature really does exist, but exists in large numbers, exists in every community, and lives right out in the open with the rest of us. They are the most devious and harmful troublemakers in our communities, yet they are often celebrated as saviors. Of course, that is what makes them successful. To quote a rather dark observation made by Charles Baudelaire, "The loveliest trick of the devil is to persuade you he does not exist." If you really want to kill your community you can skip over the initiative to not cooperate, slide on past the desire to compete and move right on to become a Volunteer Vampire.

To be a Volunteer Vampire you must seize any initiative requiring leadership and then you have to suck the life out of every idea, every action and every person who could cause the project to be a success. In many cases I have heard the Volunteer Vampire rises to the challenge and takes on a project the community so desperately needs. He always touts himself as the ultimate champion of the drive or cause that needs to be realized. He rallies the troops, he builds a team, and he is virtually inseparable from the project itself. He has a dedicated base of supporters who proclaim the greatness of the Vampire and often assert that if the project can't be done by him then it can't be done at all. From that moment on, as community volunteers rally and begin work on the project, the Volunteer Vampire sucks the life out of each and every idea and drains the life out of every hopeful volunteer.

Let's use, for example, the building of a community hall. The Volunteer Vampire will champion the cause and offer to be the lead on the quest to build a community hall. A volunteer might suggest the idea of having a fundraising supper. The Volunteer Vampire, pointing out how many other events the supper would be competing against, convinces the others the idea should not even be tried. Another person may suggest an application for some government or community grants as a way of raising funds. The Volunteer Vampire will point out how long, complicated and time-consuming those forms are, how you will be competing with larger centers that pay professionals to fill out those forms and chase grants and how the energy expended on that would be fruitless. An idea may be presented to simply have a door-to-door fundraising drive, to which the Volunteer Vampire will point out people are tired of always donating to every cause that shows up on their doorstep or rings their phone each evening, as well as how the downturn in the economy means everyone is broke and has no money to spare no matter how good the cause. In other words, the very idea is foolish and the effort would be a waste of time and energy.

And so every idea and every volunteer will be picked off one at a time as though they are in some low-budget horror movie, except the deaths are slow and withering and devoid of the classical screams. The life, blood and soul of the entire project and everyone involved are sucked out by the Volunteer Vampire. The volunteers die, the energy dies, the focus dies, and eventually the project dies. However, since every argument made by the Volunteer Vampire was built on a grain of truth and every reason was very sound and logical, though negative, there is no sadness or sense of despair in the end. Rather, there is almost a sense of relief as though a diseased animal has been relieved of its earthly bonds rather than suffering a slow and painful death. No one mourns the loss of hope. In fact, it may be celebrated.

Indeed, the Volunteer Vampire is often celebrated as someone who tried against all odds to accomplish something that turned out to be impossible. I spoke in one community and did a presentation on the power of volunteers. I also pointed out how important it is to be wary of the Volunteer Vampire because he or she will suck the life out of a project and you will celebrate the death. After I spoke the community presented a 10-year volunteer service award. There seemed to be much applause and celebration. After the event I had many people whisper to me they had presented the service medal to the Volunteer Vampire of the community. They hadn't recognized it was her until after I described what the Vampire looked like, but once they heard it, they knew it was her. She volunteered so much. She volunteered to lead so often. Yet not one project she worked on ever came to fruition. She was the Volunteer Vampire, and they gave her an award for it.

Successfully killing your community often depends only on the amount of energy and time you wish to expend in achieving that goal. Passively refusing to cooperate takes very little actual work, but does require continued focus to make sure you maintain the attitude of a Lone Hyena Leader or a Road Block Roger. Aggressively competing with other organizations or communities takes more daily effort, but if you can induce a culture of destructive competition the dividends can pay off for years with little effort. If you have time on your hands and a focus for detail, becoming a Volunteer Vampire will allow you a real hands-on feel of killing your community as you suck the life and all hope out of each person, each idea, and each project intended to grow your community. This method requires both short term and long-term commitment, but in the end, if killing your community is what you seek, then you have simply got to devote the extra time required to do the job right.

Fundamentally, killing your community comes down to refusing to cooperate with anyone. Don't cooperate with other people, other service clubs, other groups or other communities. Focus on what divides you more than what unites you. Concentrate on making those little arbitrary lines in the sand the real issue. That will allow you to remain fiercely independent, and eventually you will be able to die . . . alone.

CHAPTER 8
LIVE IN THE PAST

As I said at the beginning of this book, killing your community is all about attitude. Some people will suggest if the hospital gets closed your community will die. Others suggest losing a couple of grades at your school to the neighboring town will do the job. Still others seem to suggest the survival of your community is dependent on whether or not a road is built around your town or through your town, or whether you get a new hockey arena or ball diamond. I agree those infrastructure elements are important as a foundation to build upon, but none of them, not even closing your hospital, can make a life or death difference all by itself. I have witnessed hospitals open and close and have yet to see one such event kill a community — or ensure its success, for that matter. In fact, some of the fastest growing, most successful communities I have seen don't have a hospital and never did have one. No, those elements are *not* the beginning and end of a community. The beginning and end of every community is its people and the collective attitude they have about how they define success and whether or not they want to achieve it.

Attitude is what communities live and die by, and few of those attitudes are more successful at killing a community than the one that has you always living in the past. Almost everywhere I speak and every community I have worked in, I have a conversation with someone who displays this attitude overtly, though they seldom seem to realize it. After my presentation they will approach me to talk about things from the past they believe prevent them from moving forward as a community. I ask them if they were listening to the part of the speech when I talked about living in the past. They always say, "Yes, that was excellent," and then carry on with the very thing I repeatedly suggested they should avoid. It is a common human trait to hear information we consider valuable and then apply it to everyone else we deal with in our daily lives but fail to apply it to ourselves. Self-reflection for the purpose of improvement is a hard skill to learn and even harder for the ego to accept.

People generally display "living in the past" in one of two ways. The first way is to hold on to the glory of the past. Generally people in this category see the past through a romantic, or at least nostalgic, lens that idealizes some very non-ideal elements of history. Many books and films have romanticized the Middle Ages, or the Victorian Age, or the roaring 20s, or the cool 50s. They will capture the age by capitalizing on some aspects that are interesting or colorful, while ignoring those less appealing details in order to draw the reader or watcher — or themselves — into the fantasy. The Middle Ages can look romantic, even attractive, in movies, but they often forget to portray there were infrequent opportunities for baths, rampant head lice, and an abundance of rats, which led to the Black Plague. The roaring 20s seem like an ideal and exciting time when you ignore the low wages and absence of safety measures and healthcare. Any age can be very idealized by simply removing the bad stuff.

The human mind is a powerful machine and for the sake of self-preservation has a discreet way of removing many elements of pain while saving to memory all those wonderful moments that make us smile. As a result, our own past is often a powerful picture of happiness and success and contentment. It is a romanticized movie of our own lives, in which we idealize the clothes, the cars, the houses, the friends and the good times we had. Our memories are often much less complicated than our experience of the present and our instinct about the future, so we tend to look back with fondness on the simpler days now behind us. Typically, the older we get the less we look forward to the complexities of the future and the more we long for the simplicity of our memories of the past.

We know businesses, governments and not-for profits are all changing the way they function because of the rise of social media. Marketing and communication strategies change frequently to keep up with the new challenges and opportunities. Many of us struggle to relate and adapt to new technologies because it is hard to change, it takes work to understand the new technologies and it does not always make our lives simpler, as often as it promises. Sometimes we struggle because it seems it is more of a case of technology using us, than us utilizing technology. Adapting to each new iteration is hard and seems to get harder with age. I am not just talking about techno-logical change. Everything is changing. Our politics, or economics, or social structure; our ethics, our values, our religions are all constantly changing. Adapting can be an exhausting process because we never get a chance to catch our breath. As such, there is often an unconscious desire to return to the good old days; the days when life was simpler, moral decisions were straightforward and obvious, we were all happier and our communities were strong.

We all feel this way at one time or another. Sometimes, if the feeling becomes overwhelming, it seems the only way to correct the problems we see around us is to undo some or most of the moderniza-tion and change of the last few years. I have heard people say to make our communities strong and stable for the future we need to blow up some of those great roads we built that allowed everyone to leave town to go shopping elsewhere. To make our communities strong and stable for the future we need only bring back the ice cream parlors and get rid of the giant supermarkets that took people off our streets as families and put them into buildings as consumers. To make our communities strong and stable for the future we need only bring back door-to-door milk delivery, drive-in movies and Buick Skylarks, and all will be better. I personally believe transforming our communities should begin with reintroducing the front porch, but that may be my own personal sentimentalism setting in. The fact is, we cannot simply return to the past and even if we could, I doubt everything was as dreamy and wonderful as we remember it. The world is moving and changing. Spending countless hours discussing the glory of the past distracts us from the real and meaningful discussion about the future and how our community life fits into it. That only serves to help kill our communities, as lamenting the past accomplishes nothing and just interferes with making plans to meet the challenges of the future.

People who live in the nostalgia or romance of the past are excellent at draining the energy of creative, forward thinkers. They are excellent at getting people with ideas to lose track and become defeatist in their thinking, thereby leading to failure before any project or idea gets off the ground. They convince others, sometimes unconsciously, things will never be as good as they were and there is no point in doing something new because everything only takes us farther off the track and further away from all that used to be right in our communities. Everything needs to be undone, they will claim. Such people are most adept at changing the conversation from the search for solutions for the future to a sterile fixation on the glory of yesterday, a glory often a romanticized distortion of what the past was actually like.

During one visit to a community I met a very wonderful and happy man who seemed to really like the "13 Ways to Kill Your Community" presentation I had given. He expressed how proud he was to know the future was in such good hands with young men like me. He spoke of how great his community *was*, how great it *was* to be able to spend his childhood in such a safe and happy town as his *was*, and how wonderful it *was* to have raised his children there. I assumed his age (he was 69) had led him to talk more in the past tense as he reflected on his life, and I reminded him his town still was a safe place for kids and families to grow. He smiled and said, "No, it has all changed now that some of those big stores have come to town, and there are so many strangers."

We talked at length about values and safety and happiness, and he insisted the arrival of one store in that community had led to a dozen more moving into town and setting up shop in the general vicinity; a scenario quite common these days. The man had a passion for his community and continued to volunteer in what seemed like half of the community's organizations. I felt bad for the fellow, whose entire town had changed and modernized on him in such short order and so recently — until I found out the businesses he was referring to, the ones that had changed everything so quickly from those glory days he remembered, had arrived over a decade prior to that night I spoke. It still upset him over a decade later.

I talked to numerous other people in the town that night who stayed around to chat, and many of them volunteered without prompting or leading questions from me that the elderly gentleman with whom I had talked was a beloved and kind man, but he had opposed every change that ever took place in that community for over 40 years. Yes, you read that correctly. He was never vicious in his opposition, never started petitions, or spread lies, or gathered up hate. No, he was always kind, always smiling, and always talking about how the town was losing its sense of itself, how it was losing its glory, and how each new thing, from paving a street to tearing down an old building to putting up a new sign, was a change we would regret. He had great old stories about every old building, about every old tree, even about every old person — all the little features that made people feel at home in their community. His influence carried many along with him in opposition to every improvement, every modernization, every *whatever* that was being proposed. Eventually, however, a sense of ambivalence began to develop toward his unflagging opposition to every upgrade and innovation. His fellow townspeople all loved him, but now they all ignored him.

We all recognize there is a need to adapt and change, and a time to abandon the ways of the past. Do you still farm the way your father or grandfather did, with the same equipment, the same amount of land, the same type of vehicles, and fencing, and feeders and grain bins . . . you get the point. Grocery and hardware stores don't look the same, they don't operate the same way, or sell the same products. Dentists don't practice using the same technology from past generations, thank goodness, and neither do doctors, teachers or engineers. Every business and industry has changed to adapt to new realities, or they have gone broke and they have died. That's what people began to realize about the elderly man's gentle opposition. It was opposition to the natural order of things destined to change, and constant, unselective resistance was fruitless.

Not everyone holds onto the past with visions of glory and perfection and in such a gentle manner. The majority of those who hold onto the past do so by identifying some historical wrong; they see every moment from that point forward as being a miscarriage of justice, and every moment into the future as a deliberately perpetrated mistake that will persist until the ancient wrong is fixed. While those who are merely nostalgic for the past are mistakenly viewed as harmless romantics because of their personable and often friendly demeanor, those who are looking for "justice" over a past wrong and stubbornly refuse to let it go are often overtly angry and hostile. They are the great grudge-holders who feel someone or something wronged them, and everything in their lives that has ever been bad or will go bad in the future can be tied to that one wrong. You may think I am exaggerating, but in the same community in which I met that kind old gentleman I had an extended conversation with just such a grudge-holder. While the elderly gentleman I referred to above clung to the nostalgia of the community as it had been before that first large-box business arrived and brought others with it, another person I met saw the presence of that store as a personal wrong done specifically to her.

This very angry lady suggested to me the town council had sold the land to the developer for a very low price and never gave any local business or entrepreneur an opportunity to purchase the land and then develop it. She was livid about that, and at first I believed she had every right to be. She also suggested the store had stolen customers from all of the local businesses and the local business sector in town had all but shut down, meaning there were no local business owners left to employ people in town. The anger in her eyes turned to hints of crazy as she grew ever more livid recalling the story. I simply had to research what had transpired so I could talk about another way you could kill your community. Surely, I thought, this smiling gentleman and this entrepreneurial lady had cause to be concerned and upset.

I set to work on building a story around how the arrival of this store had led to a weakening of the community, only to find out both people had told a lot of half-truths and some outright lies to me — and in all likelihood to themselves as well — for years. The community had not had a glorious past before that one store showed up and brought others with it, as the smiling man had indicated. The town had lost two major industries and for almost 20 years teetered on the brink of collapse. Young people were fleeing because there was no work, the college had closed since all the young people had left, and businesses were shutting down long before the large store arrived. The land in question was advertised three times in three years, at a steal of a price, for locals to develop. No one ever made an offer. She was angry it wasn't bought locally, but the opportunity was there many times and for many years.

Several years before my presentation in that community, one local developer started a new value-added manufacturing industry most people in town thought was a crazy idea. It grew quickly and he hired and trained a lot of young people. That attracted a lot of young families back to the community within a couple of years. As a result of the new economic activity, the box store those two people detested purchased the piece of land for full market value, not the low price suggested by the angry lady. That in turn attracted more popular stores and businesses to the community. That in turn drew in shoppers from as far as an hour away, which I was told by many local business owners brought more money to town and revitalized the small business district, which led to a new tax base that allowed lower property taxes, which encouraged many more people to choose the community to live in, which led to many new housing starts. In other words, things started to improve with the new industry and that new box store. Not according to all, however, as one nostalgic man felt a return to memories of a glorious past would be better, and another angry lady felt some wrong had been committed against her and it needed to be undone. That smiling face was compelling and hard to resist when I first heard the story. The outrage displayed by that lady was equally compelling. They made me feel angry enough to get to the bottom of the scandal. I was momentarily ashamed when I realized both of their stories were a sham and I had almost been taken in by them.

Most often we see this behavior and these attitudes manifested in comments that may seem minor. A committee is set up to work on some project and a comment is brought forward such as, "Oh that so-and-so's grandfather did something to my grandfather 42 years ago, so there's no way I can work with them ... " There is always the very popular, "His father's uncle was a bit of a thief and a liar back in the 50s so if I were you I wouldn't trust him." Or the most common, "Why should I help with that project? What did you/they/he/she/the community ever do for me?" That type of attitude is very prevalent in many communities. It is always centered on some long-held anger and a sense life isn't fair and you have been wronged in some way. If you are trying to build a strong community, that sort of attitude ensures there is no sense of common ground on which to build. If you are trying to kill your community, on the other hand, that is exactly the sentiment you need to encourage.

I was at a meeting in a community to gather ideas about how to improve upon and build our communities for the rural development report I was writing. As usual I had invited a mixed group of about 20 people from all walks of life so we could have a free discussion on a multitude of topics. The report covered health, education, community infrastructure, economic development, youth, seniors, Aboriginals, tourism, arts and culture, water, infrastructure, transportation and trade, and the environment. We were working on ideas and trying to discuss ways things could be improved when a man stood up and yelled at me, "Nothing will get better until natural gas prices are reduced." I suggested that was a legitimate issue but it should not stop us from talking about all the other issues that could and should be discussed now about the future of our communities. He interrupted, "No, nothing you do will make one bit of difference until you fix that natural gas situation." Natural gas pricing had been de-regulated 20 years earlier and this seemed to be a thorn in his side as we tried to discuss other issues. Finally I had to ask the gentleman to leave, as his outbursts and anger were distracting from the purpose and focus of the meeting, and he would not let us move on.

Another gentleman at another meeting a few years later found his own way to distract from the community's discussion about its future. As the community and town council were gathered in the midst of a great discussion about ideas, he rose from his chair to announce in dramatic fashion he would not work with council because of a corrupt business decision that had cost taxpayers $56,000 — money that was never recovered — and then he walked out of the room. Understandably, it unsettled the room. People wanted to know what he was talking about. At one point the mayor stood to confirm he didn't know what the man had been referring to. You know how politics works these days. Some angry folks began yelling, "Cover-up!" and "What are you hiding?" Some people just have to believe the worst. It took the rest of the meeting to get everyone to calm down and focus, which left no time to discuss the community's future. Afterwards, I did some research to see what that gentleman had been referring to. It turns out the situation he was referring to had indeed happened . . . in 1972, the same year I was born. In fact, I confirmed everyone who was on council at that time had since died. There wasn't even anyone left alive to apologize for what had happened and there was no way for the situation to be fixed, but that was exactly what he wanted. It wasn't about fixing the problem, it was about holding onto it and trying to make sure everyone else held onto it. It was about making everyone as angry as him.

Still a third person, who happily acknowledged having read and appreciated this book, nevertheless spent every ounce of energy at a meeting living in the past. I was conducting a session for the community about handling its tremendous growth and what plans it should have in place to meet continued growth. The issue of health care services and seniors housing arose, so we discussed how the community could attract those much needed services and infrastructure investments. A very successful businessman steadily interrupted and criticized the choice to build a seniors housing facility and hospital in a neighboring community 28 years prior. He even recognized that 30 years ago the other community was much larger, it was the central hub of the region and it was the place where the seniors lived. Yet, for almost half an hour he complained his community didn't have its fair share and had been neglected for 30 years. He even acknowledged his community had really only come into existence in the last few years thanks to a surge in growth. I tried to turn the discussion to how great the community was doing and how they needed to focus on their future, but each time he would return to what he considered were wrongs done to him and his community for the last 30 years. I finally lost my patience and told him he was simply being angry and critical, and wasting everyone's valuable time. Not one point he had brought up could right the past, and not one word he said contributed to the community's future. I told him we were there to meet about solutions and ideas, and he could offer some up or remain quiet. He glared at me . . . quietly . . . the rest of the meeting.

In all three cases the people involved were doing an exceptionally good job of stopping us from talking about anything that dealt with the present or the future. They wanted to discuss the past and nothing else. They wanted to prevent everyone else in the room from thinking about the future, about future developments, about solutions and options, about what might come, and about how to transform their communities. All they wanted was to talk about what they felt were injustices from the past. They knew they couldn't fix the past, but the truth of the matter is they didn't really want it fixed. They had held onto the anger too long to let it go. Their entire lives had been held ransom by their anger, and they would not know how to move on even if the issues were resolved. They needed their anger to function. It had become part of their identities and letting it go would have meant letting go of part of themselves.

Wrongs have always been committed and mistakes have always been made, and that will always be the case whenever people set out to accomplish something. My grandpa used to say the only time you don't make a mistake is when you do nothing. As much as we need to correct the wrongs, at some point we need to move on to discuss solutions, not talk incessantly about what wrong was committed. Mistakes happen, but solutions don't make themselves happen. You have to work on solutions for the future, and that only happens when you let go of the past. Get on with fixing it or forgetting it, so you can get on with the future. After all, the future of our communities across North America is at stake, not their past.

The attitude that causes someone to live in the past, whether it is holding on to the idea of some glorified utopia, or holding on to some injustice that must be righted before anyone can move ahead, is intended to keep everyone looking in the wrong direction. That type of thinking is a distraction from the project, initiative or investment that will help build your community's future. There is an anonymous quote that reads, "Forget the past. No one becomes successful in the past." It is a valuable quote to hold on to. If you want to kill your community, live in the past, and you and your community are sure to become part of the past; a distant, nostalgic, forgotten, memory in the dustbin of history.

CHAPTER 9
SHUT OUT YOUR SENIORS

Seniors are an important element in any society and their importance grows, as do their numbers. In many cultures around the world seniors are revered for the wisdom and the experiences they hold. Most of us, however, tend to view our seniors as just easy-going and cordial folks. They are rarely given due consideration when it comes to planning for the future. They are often viewed as relics of the past. Don't be fooled. They are a dangerous group, and under the right circumstances can cause a riot of success within your community. Seniors hold a lot of assets in greater abundance then the average citizen in the general population. They have tremendous knowledge and experience many of us have yet to acquire, but all of it is there for us to glean if we only ask. They also generally have acquired a degree of wealth intended to help them enjoy their newly-found freedom upon retirement. As well, that freedom gives them more time in their daily lives than many in the average population possess. Knowledge, experience, wealth and time are all critical elements in building a successful community. Given seniors have all of these elements in abundance is what makes them dangerous, which means you must do everything in your power to relegate them to the sidelines to ensure the failure of your community.

Most communities have a small group of people who sit on the town or county councils, run their businesses or work their jobs, coach sports teams, lead charitable organizations, volunteer at the school, mentor scouts, put away the chairs at church, and a myriad of other roles and responsibilities in some combination. As an elected official, I was always impressed how often I would meet with different groups at different times over different issues, and how often the same people from the community would be in attendance at each and every meeting. I would often finish one meeting with a group over an issue in the community, walk down the street to another venue with another group on another issue, only to discover almost all the same people were working on that issue as well.

I refer to those people as the STPs — the Same Ten People. They are the tireless, diehard, dedicated folks in your community who fill just about every vacancy they come across in the community. Some critics accuse them of being too dominant or of "running the town," and on occasion that can be the case. More often than not, however, I found they were simply dedicated and determined, and when no one else steps up to do the job, they take it upon themselves. Without those STPs it seems the community wouldn't be much of a community at all. It demonstrates just how significant community volunteers are to your community. Many of our seniors were those STPs at one time.

When seniors retire the first thing they find they have in abundance is time, which so often makes them great volunteers. Most of the rest of us are still working one or two jobs, raising the kids, running them to all sorts of events, volunteering in some community organizations, and so on. Seniors have freed themselves from many of those bonds. They don't have to work full time, if at all. Their kids are grown. Their job is done. Now they have some time off to enjoy all those things they promised themselves they would do once they weren't so busy with the daily grind of life. Some had planned on traveling more, or golfing more, or spending more time with their grandkids. Whatever it is they planned to do, they will go do it, at least for a while. It usually isn't long before they are back in the community and wanting to be involved again. Some will be back because of health reasons, or homesickness, or the need to be close to grandkids. Others will be back because there is only so much time you can spend traveling or golfing. Some decide, after some time away, that relaxing and retiring are more of a part-time than full-time enterprise. Regardless, when they come back, they will be looking for something to do in your community. That is how they become dangerous.

They will want to help and volunteer. Most would, in fact, be honored to be asked to volunteer on committees or boards, or with projects in the community. Our seniors have worked their entire lives to build their businesses, their homes, their families and their communities. They were the original STPs, and once an STP, always an STP. They want to keep building for their grandchildren and great-grandchildren. For some, volunteering will be motivated by a sense of pride to carry on what they helped build over the years. For others, it may be a sense of obligation remaining from those amazing days when communities were built and strengthened by the people in them, not by government programs. Most will want to volunteer because of the social interactions they don't get as often as they would like since they retired. We are social beings who crave social interactions for our own mental and physical health. All of those who volunteer will do so because they want to be useful and they want to feel needed. We all do. Sometimes, however, seniors don't know what to do to help, they don't know where they fit in, or they feel like they are not needed or wanted. Some seniors are like youth in that they need to be asked seven times before they really believe you want them to help out. But often, all it takes is a phone call asking them if they are willing to help, and they will turn up in droves, making their voices heard and making new and meaningful contributions wherever you let them.

Successful communities often capture that senior resource and have an excellent senior volunteer base for many functions and organizations. Some communities have gone as far as hiring a volunteer coordinator or community organizer to identify, recruit and match volunteers with the appropriate organization. The coordinator helps see to it volunteers' time is properly managed, the experience is socially engaging, the greatest efficiency possible is achieved and volunteers are not burning out. That is particularly important to seniors who want to do something enjoyable and want opportunities to visit and meet new people, but don't want to be over-used or abused. The last volunteer coordinator I interviewed didn't just work on getting the best use out of the time seniors devoted, however. He saw real advantages and success arise from his initiative to build cross-generational teams. He found he got the most success by combining youth with seniors in volunteer organizations. Sometimes he would mix the middle generation into the fold, but he said the best results came from putting that mid-something generation together on their own committee. In fact, the committees would sometimes playfully compete to see who could get work done faster, with the committee of young and old always beating the committee of middle-age volunteers.

There seems to be a natural complement between the energy the younger generation possesses and the wisdom of the older generation. It makes them very effective together. It is as though the young respect the wisdom of the old, and the old respect the energy of the young, more so than either respect the energy or wisdom of the mid-somethings. There has always been a natural allegiance between grandkids and grandparents. We have all seen how much more our kids listen to their grandparents' stories and advice than they do to ours, and we have all seen how much more appreciative grandparents are of the exuberance of their grandkids than they were of their children's energy. There is a natural alliance there that makes them an effective team in your community. Communities that build those types of volunteer teams build success.

There is though an important aspect of that alliance that spreads beyond simply building effective volunteer teams, and that is the abundance of knowledge and experience possessed by seniors referred to earlier in the chapter. Transferring knowledge and experience links the generations together by building a shared appreciation for where you have come from *and* support for where you are going. Grandkids learn about their family histories more often from their grandparents than from their parents. Grandparents have the time to teach their grandkids more about life, and the grandkids listen more than they would when their parents tell the same stories. Parents are often so insanely busy with their "tyranny of the urgent" lives, however, they sometimes forget to relay their stories even when their kids are ready to listen. When volunteering in community groups, grandparents talk a lot about the community and its history and tell stories to the grandchild generation that help explain the world of the present by describing where the community has come from and what it has been through. Grandparents have patience they didn't have when they were younger and will happily take the time to relay experiences to the grandchildren in a way that helps them avoid pitfalls as they work on projects or committees, and the grandchild generation listens and learns in ways they simply can't or won't with their parents.

Likewise, grandparents often support the desire of their grandkids to try new things and seek new adventure more than they typically did with their kids. As parents, their job was to make their kids strong and smart and get them off on the right foot for life. Once they are grandparents, their grandchildren are wonderful, and innocent, and already smart and strong, and must be allowed to try new things and be children. Our perspectives change as we age. The pressure we have as parents to raise good kids gets exchanged for an optimism when we are older that the grandkids can do no wrong. Grandkids come up with all kinds of new and energetic ideas they want to try and the grandparent generation laughs and says, "Let's try that." Perhaps those two generations become so supportive of each other because there is a generation in between those two that serves as a common enemy. Regardless, there is and has long been a link between those two generations. Your community can be made stronger with the exchange of experience and wisdom for energy and new ideas. Your community can be made stronger when its past and future are brought together to work on today.

We have discussed how seniors have a greater abundance of time, knowledge and experience than those in the average population. They don't have kids to raise or full-time jobs to work, so they have more time on their hands than the currently serving full-time STPs who are sprinting through a hectic life of obligations. They also have a lot of experiences and knowledge from a lifetime of tries that sometimes led to failure and sometimes led to success. If we could just glean that knowledge we could save ourselves from making some grave mistakes. Seniors, however, have also been saving (at least most of them have) for their retirement so they can afford to enjoy life, so they have also tended to accumulate some wealth. I want you to understand right now I am not suggesting seniors are obliged to invest in every hare-brained scheme you come up with, or they must donate to every fundraising cause and event you can dream up. I am also not saying they are all wealthy, but neither are they all poor. If you read the news and listen to the media you may get the impression all seniors are destitute. That simply is not the case.

Somewhere during the last decade we have either got the impression all seniors are poor so they can't afford anything, or seniors may be wealthy but since they built this place they should get everything for free. When I hear people speak of "seniors" housing I usually discover what they mean is "affordable" housing, even though there is no reason to force those two concepts together. So I see many communities wait for the government to come along with a program to build "free/affordable/subsidized" seniors housing. All the while many seniors in the community can and will pay for the housing they need, (although some seniors who can afford it still want it for free if the government is willing to pay for it . . . as would you). What they need is not affordable housing, but appropriate housing.

Many seniors in our communities live in housing that is old and not modernized. That doesn't pose a problem except that older designs, even when renovated, will often still have a lot of stairs and narrow doorways inappropriate for older people with bad knees or weaker legs, and completely inappropriate for anyone who requires a walker or wheelchair for mobility. As well, most of those seniors who raised families within those houses now find they have far too much space to heat and clean now with only one or two people in the house. Potential reduced mobility issues are further amplified by large yards that require regular maintenance such as weeding and mowing in the summer, and sidewalks and driveways that need shoveling in the winter. Many of our seniors find themselves in homes that have become inappropriate for them. Many have also found themselves in homes with good equity they are willing to use if the right housing is available.

I worked in one community, not too many years ago, which was literally in the throes of death. The population was in rapid decline, the attitude of the remaining population was caustic and businesses were closing up shop each month. It was presumed by everyone the community was simply going to die a slow and painful death, until one day a local entrepreneur came up with an idea that had the potential to transform the entire face of that community with one development project. The entrepreneur had observed too many of his aunts, uncles and family friends were struggling with inappropriate housing as they aged. They couldn't handle owning a house anymore, but since nothing appropriate for seniors was available, they were forced to move out of the community, one by one. The entrepreneur asked seniors about their willingness to buy in town, rather than move away, and compiled a list of interested people who would commit to buying if the project was built. These people were not old and infirm. They did not need hospital care. They were newly retired people who didn't want to mow lawn and shovel snow, or do a lot of maintenance on a house that was too big for them now. They wanted a place they knew would be safe if they went away for a few months on vacation. They wanted a place with neighbors like themselves with whom they could mingle when they were home the rest of the year. So the entrepreneur decided to build seniors' appropriate condos.

This story should have immediately had a happy ending. This was the largest development project ever to be undertaken in that community. It wasn't even that large, at just 20 units, but the construction value and the potential to keep seniors in the community, along with their time, experience, knowledge and wealth had huge value. Just as the project appeared to be ready to launch, just as enough seniors had committed to the project and were excited by the idea of being able to live in a seniors-appropriate condo complex in their town, the project was derailed by one lone voice. A leader in the community stood up at a meeting on the project and objected. "How is this seniors housing? The government should be doing this. Why are seniors being forced to pay for their own place?" That was all she said. She followed up with a letter to the local paper, and because she was on town council she introduced a motion that the town not support the project. That motion passed.

She didn't really have the ability to stop the project, and the town's support was inconsequential, except her words got a few seniors thinking the government should be doing the project and it should be subsidized, and so mere days later two couples withdrew their commitment to buy. Even if there had been a government program available it would take years to get such a project approved and those seniors would never get the opportunity to have the housing they wanted in their community when they needed it. The fact remains there was, and still is, no government program to build such a project. There were only programs for those seniors who wouldn't be able to afford the rent, not programs for such large capital outlays on projects that are better undertaken by private developers.

On a project that is 20 units, having two units unsold means the entire profit margin is gone. The project should have been dead. Acquiring a project of that size in a community of 1200 people would have been a huge boon to the local economy, especially when it meant seniors, and their wealth, could stay in the community. That entrepreneur was ridiculously committed to turning the town's fortunes around, so he continued to try to sell the last two units. Within a couple of years a new council was elected to town and the entrepreneur began to make headway once again. Just when things were looking promising, however, a new group sprung up and protested the project would block their view of the golf course, so once again the project was delayed. This went on for seven years. For seven years people in town wanted their seniors to stay in the community, wanted them to have appropriate housing, but for seven years group after group prevented the project from being built. It was a model of madness.

Finally, after seven years, the project was completed. Almost immediately the benefits were apparent. Closed-down businesses began to re-open and new businesses were starting up as seniors stayed to live, to require new services and to spend money in the community. Young families were moving into town to start those new businesses. The town couldn't yet afford to create new subdivisions to house the new families that were arriving, but that wasn't a problem. The newcomers were moving into the homes previously owned by the seniors who had now moved into the condos. Everything was working out well. There was an air of hope and excitement in the community, like they had finally turned the corner — at least for a short time.

People began to talk about how the demand for another complex of similar nature was mounting and needed to be built in town. All the units in the current complex had been sold, so a new wave of retirees and seniors had no place in town to buy. They were going to have to move out of the community. The community wondered aloud, "Who will build the next complex?" Once the discussion of building another 20-unit building was heard, the protests started up again just as fiercely as before. The same old arguments reared from the same old, ugly heads. People in the community asked the same entrepreneur to build again. He said, "No." He had worked seven years on that project without possibility of making a dime. They asked other developers, but none of them would build in that community because of the protests. The community hadn't learned even though the evidence was right in front of them. Meanwhile, new seniors left for towns that had condo units appropriate for them. They continue to do so and they take their time, their experience and knowledge, and their wealth with them when they go.

In this context I recall a great discussion I had with a couple in their late 60s who lived in one of North America's largest and fast-est-growing cities, Calgary. They had purchased their house 45 years earlier for less than one-fifth of what it was currently worth. Now their children had moved out and lived in communities all across the continent. They lamented how they used to know all their neighbors, they used to pay much less in property taxes, there used to be less crime in their neighborhood and they used to be able to golf without an expensive membership at the local golf club. They had outgrown the size and style of their beloved home, their neighborhood and their city.

It was like a revelation to them when I spoke of the dozens and dozens of communities not far from their current location that had condo-style living ideal for seniors, where they wouldn't have to mow the lawn or shovel snow and they could still grow their garden as they had for decades. They wanted to move into a senior-appropriate condo, but they were not aware communities just outside the city had beautiful places available for a fraction of the price they would pay in their current vicinity. Add to that the much lower property taxes, and beautiful, underutilized golf courses with very reasonable membership costs where you can usually just walk on instead of booking a time, and they were very intrigued. The clincher in the discussion occurred when I discussed the friendly nature of these communities, where they would get to know their neighbors, where they could feel safe and secure, in a place that was better suited for their speed, and where they would be welcomed.

I got a call from them a few months later informing me they had actually taken the plunge and moved. I was surprised and delighted. The community was farther from the city than I'd imagined they would venture, but I was not surprised by the community they chose. With the equity out of their home they were able to buy two condos; one in Arizona for the winter months, and one in a small town in Alberta, Canada for the summer months. As regions, Alberta and Arizona rank as having the greatest number of sunny days on the continent, but as communities they were offering services this couple was seeking. They had incredible walk-on access to a beautiful and affordable golf course in a quiet place with other seniors who all liked to do something they hadn't done in years: square dancing. Yes, square dancing. Both communities where they bought condos offered square dancing and they loved it. On top of all that they had warm weather year-round, no lawn to mow, no snow to plow, all in secured neighborhoods with people their own age. They hadn't realized what kind of life was available to them if they were willing to look beyond their street. They are still very happy and active and they still send me a Christmas card every year.

The community in Alberta they moved to was, at one time, barely hanging on. That community had also built a seniors-appropriate condo development similar to the other community, but this community didn't protest or expect the government to do it for them. As a result, what happened next with this community was nothing short of amazing. A couple of units from that first project were sold to people from outside the community because when those outsiders saw these units were available at such a great price and right next to the golf course, they decided to move. Eventually word spread about the price of the units, their amazing layout, and their proximity to the golf course, as well as all the other services the seniors wanted that were offered in the community. Then local residents, as well as people from other communities, began enquiring about future developments. Another development went up. And then another. The third development is when the Calgary couple moved in.

A new clubhouse was built on the golf course, a new restaurant opened in town, and other businesses opened as more and more seniors moved in. A sense of excitement began to grow as increasing numbers of people recognized that new opportunities were opening up in the community. The next step in the community's re-growth, which was something no one foresaw, was the influx of young families that began moving to the community. Some moved there to be closer to parents and grandparents. Others moved there because they heard about the job and business opportunities that were sprouting up. The town grew and developed into a place of opportunity for every generation and developed a culture of capitalizing on opportunity and celebrating success. These, of course, are the forces you have to fight against in your campaign to kill your community.

Some communities make the mistake of thinking they can get away with only building seniors housing, while not providing any quality-of-life aspects for seniors. Those communities believe the seniors will simply vanish into their condos to play crib and shuffleboard until they die. Wrong. I warned you at the beginning of this chapter — once an STP, always an STP. They will sneak out, they will volunteer, they will spend money and they will build your community. If they stay they will make a difference. They are the foundation of your community and they want to help keep it strong. If you really want to kill your community you must be certain seniors have no appropriate housing so they must leave, and they will take their wisdom, their experience and their money with them. With no foundation, your community can crumble.

CHAPTER 10
REJECT EVERYTHING NEW

The implicit nature of human beings is to strive and work to achieve consistency because in consistency there is security. As we age, this tendency grows and we become increasingly willing to trade opportunity and rewards for security and consistency. On occasion the need for these values becomes so strong we willingly endure a harsh and bitter reality rather than take a risk to improve our fortunes. We tend to prefer the devil we know over the one we don't. This means we choose not to try new food, or new drinks, or new friends, or new places, or new ideas. We become entrenched in the status quo and what we know. As communities we often choose not to accept new people, or new ideas, or new ways of thinking, or new attitudes. We reject everything that is new and opt to keep the familiar devil, the slow deterioration of our community, because we fear change even if change means success.

When I was first elected, in April of 2002, I was a bouncing baby politician open to all sorts of new ideas, adventures, experiences and opportunities. I worked incredibly hard. I was single, so I almost lived in my car as I traveled crazy miles and crazy hours all over a huge constituency getting to know everyone and every issue. My parents got a bit concerned about me around October when I looked a little run down even though I was revving and pulsing with excitement and energy. They insisted I plan for a break over the Christmas holidays and get away somewhere I could relax, or they were going to get me a ticket to join them and their friends at a resort in Mexico. I said I would take care of my own holiday plans, but I got busy and forgot. True to their word they presented me with an envelope when I showed up at Christmas. Enclosed was a ticket to accompany them and their friends to a resort in Mexico . . . and a bill. They never suggested they were paying for the trip, just that I was going.

My parents are fantastic people who are still really quite young. We get along very well, and I know and like all their friends, so I was actually looking forward to the holiday. We did a lot of touring around the countryside and the communities, sampled the culture and the food at local festivals, lounged in the sun by the pool, and generally had a lot of fun. Well, we all had fun except one gentleman. He expressly did not like the Mexican beach, the Mexican sun, the Mexican food, the Mexican culture, and not even the Mexican beer. Honestly, he was pretty down on everything about the trip. I wondered why he was even there. I asked my dad one evening why a guy who seemed to dislike everything about Mexico had bothered to go there in the first place.

My dad explained the man actually wanted to try to do something different, but because he'd never ventured beyond the sight of the water tower back home he had no idea what was in store for him. I suddenly had a very clear picture of a man who had literally never lost sight of the water tower. I could actually picture him driving away, eyes always quickly and frequently glancing to the rearview mirror, and the moment the water tower disappeared from sight he turned the car around and went home. Obviously, that wasn't to be taken literally, but it was a great metaphor that stuck in my mind. He had never really sampled anything different his entire life. He spent 64 years working tirelessly on the farm doing the same old same old. He had difficulty opening his mind to such a new situation and new environment. I'm not blaming him. It was bound to be incredibly difficult for him to enjoy trying something new. So, he was stuck grumbling about how he didn't like "it" and "it" was everything that was different. The interesting thing about his story is that he kept traveling and kept trying new things and now he is a constant traveler who loves the adventure. It demonstrates it is never too late to learn and appreciate something new.

I was reminded of this story some years later as I was giving a speech that included some very off-the-wall ideas for igniting a fire in rural communities. I had finished the speech and was taking questions from the floor when one man raised his hand and said, "You can't really expect us to try one of those ideas you mentioned?" I shrugged and told him he could try something else if he wanted to, and then asked him why he didn't think the community could try one of those ideas. He said with complete candor and sincerity, "Well, we have never tried them before." Yes, he said those exact words. My mind instantly flashed to Mexico and a man who had never tried anything new and wasn't about to start now. I tried to hide the insidious smirk on my face as I reminded him of a quote often attributed to Albert Einstein; "The definition of insanity is doing the same thing over and over again and expecting different results each time." Why not give something new a shot, especially since the tried and true ideas haven't succeeded?

I felt bad for the gentleman visiting Mexico because he hadn't experienced other cultures when he was younger and very likely had not tried anything new in decades. Then I found myself thinking about the difference between people who never *had* the chance to experience other cultures and people who never *took* that chance to experience other cultures. Both live in very small worlds with little variation in their experiences, which means they are both ignorant of the diversity of life and lifestyles around the globe. The first, however, is a victim of circumstance because the choice is not theirs, much like the elderly gentleman who'd never had a previous chance to go to Mexico. The other, the one who has the opportunity to try new cultures and experiences but refrains, is the engineer of their own ignorance. Historically it is conceivable many of our small communities are victims of circumstance. They never had exposure to thoughts and ideas that went beyond the water tower, but in today's day and age, keeping your thoughts, your ideas and your knowledge within immediate sight range of the water tower means deliberately engineering failure.

In terms of rural development and community growth, historically many communities refused to share information and stories with one another about their successes and failures, for fear of the competition it would create. Even if they were willing to share there was little way for the ideas to spread, and so there was very little information available to assist communities looking for ideas. Communication was very poor compared to what it is now. Younger readers will probably not realize only two generations ago many farmers and rural residents did not have phones, or if they did they were "party" lines. There was no web, no social media and no real- time news. On the day of my first election victory we still used small flip phones that could store up to 10 phone numbers . . . that was it. The world was huge and information pockets were small at best, if you could even locate them.

Technology has grown exponentially over the last decade and the information we have available is occasionally overwhelming if we don't know how to sift through it. Now we have instant, free video-com- munication to and from the rest of the world. I can video-conference with friends in Germany for free. I can view towns' websites and search out success stories from around the world all day long. In fact, communities are setting up websites to post their own success stories and their proven models for long-term prosperity because they want to advertise and market themselves to businesses, to families and to the world about how great and successful their community has become. There are rural development institutes that perform research on the viability of communities and rural economic regions in coun- tries all over the world, and they pass that research on to whoever wants to read it. At one time we couldn't get the information we needed, just like that man who didn't have the option to go to Mexico for most of his life. But now the information is there, and we simply need to glean value from it. To choose not to know, when it is all right there for the taking, is to willfully be ignorant of possible solutions and to deliberately choose to have your community fail.

I'm reminded of a friend from my first year of university. We became great friends when we both failed out of our first year, and the following year found ourselves at the same college working on redemption. We did a lot of studying together the second year and spent a lot of time hanging out, except for the spring break week. He went off to some spring break town to have a good time and I went home to work on the farm. When we got back he very enthusiastically and passionately told me how he was going to quit school and start his own business and make a lot of money, and I should get into business with him. He was very excited. He explained he had found the perfect business idea when he was on vacation.

The spring break period at our college didn't quite coincide with the spring break from other institutions so my friend had a few quiet days in the community to look around after the parties were all over and the students left town to return to school. He explained how he was sitting on a patio one afternoon and noticed the business across the street was as busy after the students had left town to return to school as when they were there. In his words, "People were going in there steadily to spend money, and it didn't seem to matter what was going on or what time of day it was." He realized the community he was visiting for spring break was quite similar to the one he planned on living in back home. He explained to me how they were of similar size and demographic distribution, and they had a similar economic base, yet the community back home did not have a business at all like the one he was watching from the patio. His notion was to set up the same business at home. If it works there, he reasoned, it had to work back home.

He took the idea and headed home to begin his new enterprise. It has been a huge success for him, and for the community he built it in. Now he has several different businesses in several different communities, all successful. Between golf games and vacations overseas he travels throughout the U.S. and Canada identifying businesses that are stellar successes within a specific type of community. He then seeks out similar communities that lack that proven successful business, and opens just such a business himself. He always does his homework correctly and completely, and has a flawless record of success. On occasion it brought a sigh to my lips when I climbed back into my five-year-old Chevrolet Impala after a cup of coffee with him and watched him drive off in his very nice, very new Jaguar. I used to lament that moment I turned down the opportunity to join him in his business

venture, but I have since learned we all have roles to play and mine is
to help communities find success, because that is where my passion
leads me. Always pursue your passion.

Every time we have coffee he reminds me his realization that
day on the patio was not about the successfulness of that particular
business, but about how successes were all around him, staring him
in the face. His insight was that many wonderfully creative people
had taken risks to try out something new and all he had to do was
learn from their success and mimic it elsewhere. He never credited
himself with being brilliant and innovative, but he did credit himself
with being resourceful and bold. That he was. You could criticize him
for not being original, but ideas are borrowed all the time. The first
people with ideas for a grocery store, a hardware store, and a pharmacy
had their ideas borrowed and then improved upon. Such practices are
common in business. The only real difference in this case is that the
borrowed and slightly improved-upon models were set up in a location
where there was no competition, and in a place where it was quite clear
the business would be successful. One of my favorite quotes comes
from him: "They say we should learn from our failures if we can. It is
even smarter to learn from other people's failures to save yourself the
pain. Personally, I find it much more prudent and profitable to learn
from other people's successes."

There are stories of success from communities all over the world
eager to share their experiences. They're there for you to see — you
simply have to be willing to try something new. It doesn't have to be
some radically different idea never before tried — why take the risk
when there are so many different ideas that have already been proven
successful and simply need to be slightly modified and adapted to your
particular community? If you're a medium-size community that sits
at the edge of a mountain range, for instance, and you are wondering
about ways to make improvements, there are bound to be any number
of communities similar to yours that have tried and succeeded with
ideas you would never have dreamed of yourself, but could work very
successfully for you. It doesn't matter if you are large or small, near a
lake, on the prairie, surrounded by forest, or situated on a river. Some

community maybe thousands of miles away is in a similar situation and has tried and succeeded with ideas that will work for you. All you need is a computer, some patience, and a willingness to try something new.

This does not mean you should completely give up on looking for truly new ideas unique to your community. Of course, you may discover something absolutely no community on Earth (at least that you know of) has ever tried before. It is always worth a shot to try something new when you have confirmed everything you have tried before has not worked. Presenting new ideas for consideration may possibly make you a target of ridicule and criticism, but you have got to be willing to take the risk if you want the reward. Every great and wonderful invention, every discovery, every idea or change in the course of human history, whether it was global or local, originated with someone who was ready to try something different. If no one tried anything different or took a chance because they could fail or be ridiculed, then nothing would ever change. It would be status quo until the end of time.

When I was a high school student I was invited to participate in a series of three discussions about the future of the community. Throughout the second meeting we were discussing ideas for attracting people and their money. It was nearing the end of the meeting before I finally built up my courage to offer what I believed to be a meritorious idea. The town I grew up in is a very lovely little community that sits bravely in the middle of a massive expanse of table-top prairie. I cautiously raised my hand and offered up tourism as an idea to attract people and money to the community. A much more experienced and older gentleman snickered and bleated, "What are they going to come and do? Watch the dog run away for three days?" His put-down wasn't meant to insult me but rather the supposedly un-alluring environment in which our community was located. Regardless, it hit me hard and I sat meekly and made no comment the rest of the meetings.

I had the notion someone, somewhere in such a large world would want to see something we had to offer. I was also convinced if just the occasional busload of people showed up and walked around snapping a few pictures, then others in the town would start to wonder what these people found so interesting. I thought perhaps if a few tourists took an interest in the community, some of the people in town might begin to appreciate it a bit more. Rarely do we appreciate what we have until someone else appreciates it. There would be nothing like a few tourists stopping in every week, taking pictures, talking, and pointing to remind everyone in town what they have is of interest to other people in the world and should not be taken for granted.

I did not know exactly how or why tourists would come to the community, but I thought it was a worthy idea to raise at a meeting designed to dream up ideas for the community's future. I thought it was an idea that could and should be explored. If it had no merit then so be it, but it had never been considered before so it was worth a shot. I discovered much later on, after a tour through Germany, that Germans are fascinated with Western culture. A German author wrote many "Old West" books in German based on his experiences of living up and down the Continental Divide for years. It created a fascination in Germany with the "Wild West" mystique. Clubs in Germany have been formed that have Western-themed parties where people dress up as cowboys and Native Americans — but finding authentic clothes for such an occasion is almost impossible. It was presented to me by Germans at a meeting that providing those clothes would be a great business opportunity. Regular blue jeans stitched with Native American designs by Native Americans would fetch a ten-fold increase over the price of the jeans alone. I speak of the opportunity everywhere I go, but still nobody has ever taken advantage of the idea in all the years I have been doing my presentation.

After being in Germany and hearing their interest, I got home and saw things differently. I saw a frontier prairie outpost surrounded by old-fashion cowboys who run cattle and bison. I saw a town with an authentic steam train that still ran tourists up and down the old rail line. I saw a rugged river close by that offered opportunities for canoeing and hiking. I saw ranches with picturesque views of expansive, wind-swept native prairie. In fact, some of those folks in Germany talked a lot about the "space" we had. They were enthralled by the large expanses of empty terrain. Germany has 87 million people all packed into a territory half the size of Texas. I could see why they were fascinated with our space. I bet some of them would have actually been fascinated by the ability to "watch the dog run away for three days." They don't all have to come over, but really, it would only take a few to turn that small prairie town on its ear and cause the locals to wonder what the tourists saw and to perhaps appreciate what the tourists came to appreciate for themselves. That would be a great way to adjust the attitude and demonstrate there was more than nothing there to see . . . or more importantly, to demonstrate there was value in the nothingness.

I now find it humorous when an idea presented is ridiculed before it is ever explored. I imagine someone sitting on a beach complaining they don't like being made to enjoy the warm sun, the soft breeze and the cold beer because they have never tried it before. I re-visit the Germans I met, wearing cowboy hats and dreamily asking questions about what it is like to ride a horse on the open prairie with nothing but a few friends, a few cows, a dog and vistas as far as the eye can see. People who suggest trying something new are often ridiculed or resented because everyone hates change when it is first presented. After the change has occurred and everyone gets used to it, however, they act as though it has always been that way and defend against any new change again, good or bad, for the sake of securing a new status quo. Communities that seek out ideas, explore options and find partners that extend beyond the sight of the water tower often find an entirely new world of opportunities on which they can capitalize. They find the future.

Communities and people that run from new ideas out of fear, that shun opportunities that stare them right in the face from across the street, that embrace everything that's old, that reject outright anything that is new, are destined to see their community fail. People who take hold and reject anything new are easy to identify. Don't mistake their desperate arguments for anything but a desire to keep everything the same and status quo-like. They have names. Sometimes they are

NIMBYs (Not In My Back Yard) and sometimes they are NOPEs (Not On Planet Earth). They are the old breed of status quo supporters. The new breed of determined souls who reject everything new are CAVE people (Citizens Against Virtually Everything) and BANANAs (Build Absolutely Nothing Anywhere Near Anything). They don't want anything to change. The most dangerous of the new breed are the FEARS (Fire-up Everyone Against Reasonable Solutions). They yell and scream, they present lies and feelings as facts, they attack people personally so good people become afraid to speak up at meetings, and they succeed by spreading fear. They are the equivalent of social terrorists because spreading fear is how they seize control. Fighting FEARS is necessary if you are to succeed, while letting FEARS take over is a sure path to failure. Regardless of the form they take, they are a powerful lot and their sole, or perhaps soul, intent is to stop change and prevent solutions.

In the rural-community development report I wrote early in my political career I had recommended we could address both the lack of capacity in urban hospitals and the empty space in rural hospitals by offering a broader range of health services in rural centers that urbanites could use. It would utilize capacity, save infrastructure investments, lower wait times for everyone, and drive some dollars into rural communities. It was a win-win, or at least so I thought until I received one of the strangest phone calls of my political career. The caller chastised me for suggesting urbanites should come out to the country to get medical services. She didn't want them coming out. I was stunned. It got stranger yet when she told me they would want to move there because of the affordable housing, beautiful scenery, small schools, recreation facilities and such. I didn't see the problem until she yelled at me for not understanding she didn't want them to come out at all. Not to visit, and not to live. No urbanites, period.

Earlier that year she had called to tell me she was anxious to see the report because we needed a plan to keep our schools and hospitals open, our roads paved, the lights on in the arena and so on. Apparently she thought the population and the economy would continue to shrink, but all the services could continue to be delivered. I challenged her to explain to me how any government could keep the school and the hospital open, the road paved, and the lights on in the arena when there weren't enough people to use them or pay the taxes to support them. I challenged her to explain how keeping people out of town was going to make the town a viable place. She paused for a brief time, said two final words that were not "good-bye," and hung up the phone.

I was sure I had just borne witness to some bizarre psychotic break and was wondering if I should advise appropriate authorities on the matter. Since then I have realized she didn't comprehend how utterly illogical her position was, but she also was not the only one of her kind. I have seen many other people make equally illogical arguments over the ensuing years. They want their way of life and services, which are at risk because of the status quo, but they don't want anything to change. The irony of the matter is that everything changes. The world is change. It always will be. You can watch it, understand it, internalize it, respond to it, adapt to it, adopt it, regulate it, take part in it, capitalize on it and make it your own . . . or you can deny it is happening, ignore its consequences, and it will hit you like a freight train. Change will come whether you like it or not. Many have tried to fight it — none have succeeded for long. Change always wins.

If failure of your community is what you are after, don't consider any new ideas. Abandon the notion of taking a risk with something unproven because the chance something might happen to change the course of your town's future for the better is too great. Better to accept the slow, painful death of same old same old. If failure of your community is what you seek you should especially turn away from any ideas that have already proven to be a success in other places. Those types of ideas come with little risk and high reward and could easily transform your community. Reject anything new. Any new building, any new development, any new concept, or idea, or suggestion should be heartily rejected with passionate arguments that what you have and what you are is all you ever need, as you erect higher and higher walls to separate you from anything beyond sight of the water tower. With proper focus and dedication, your community can slowly go insane and die doing exactly what it has always done.

CHAPTER 11
IGNORE OUTSIDERS

In previous chapters we have discussed the qualities and values specific groups bring to your community. Youth bring energy and ideas. Seniors often bring time and money. Those are not the only two groups who are important to ignore if you are looking to bring about failure, however. There are many other groups who bring attributes and skills to your community that can make it stronger and ensure its enduring prosperity. One of the most powerful groups is made up of the outsiders. They are people who have deliberately chosen to locate in your community, and as such they are often determined to see your community succeed. If you wish to kill your community it is important to identify and mark them as outsiders and ensure they always stay outsiders.

Outsiders, or as they are referred to in some places I have visited — "come-from-aways" — have many common traits, but they are not one distinct group. An outsider is anyone who does not identify with your community's shared general sense of who it is. Outsiders can be from a different and distinct cultural group, they may speak a different language, they may have a different history or religion, they often live a different lifestyle or eat different food, or they may simply not originate from your community. I am going to highlight three different classifications of outsider groups in this chapter for the sake of clarification and brevity.

The first classification of outsider denotes people who come from a country outside the North American continent. They are usually the most different from the local community population, and therefore are the least understood.

The second classification includes those people who arrive from another community within North America. They aren't as different as the members of the first classification, but they don't know the community history or the way the community likes to "do things around here," so they tend to remain outsiders. Those two groups bring wholly different new strengths to a community because of where they came from and their motivation for moving, but they still have much in common because they are, literally, outsiders.

Members of the third classification of outsiders are distinct from the first two classes because they are in the unique position of having originally been *insiders* within the community. They become outsiders because they do not fit into the collective character and accepted mindset of the community. They often think differently, choose interesting career paths, or have non-typical lifestyles. I am sure you are thinking of some obvious examples. For instance, young people in a small town who dress gothic or have multiple piercings, or perhaps someone who decides to be a glass-blower or a tattoo artist in a small agricultural community, or perhaps someone who is gay in a very perceptibly hetero community. Don't limit your thinking to those stereotypical examples, however. This group could include a farmer who decides to raise bison instead of beef, or grow canary seed instead of corn. It could be someone who builds a net-zero house, or travels to exotic places in their free time. It is simply anyone whose lifestyle choices run against common practice.

Such people often have a long family history in the community and have automatic admission to the insiders' club at birth. As they increasingly go against the grain, however, their membership gets put up for review. To be sure, this is not a process that happens overnight. As they do things, think things or say things out of the norm, casual conversations begin about how different they are from the community. The more different they are, the faster the momentum builds. No one can ever say for sure when or how the membership into the insiders' club gets revoked, but we have all seen it happen. One day you are an insider with all the special status and privilege that goes with it, and then one day you aren't. Some of those Third Order Outsiders will stick around the community and attempt to bring new perspectives and new ideas, but most of them eventually opt to leave for someplace where they feel like they belong.

The Second Order Outsiders are fellow countrymen and women who simply were not born locally. They may come from 30 miles down the road, or they may in fact come from 3000 miles across the country, but they are outsiders nonetheless. They are outsiders because often very little is known about them by you or your neighbors. They may stand out because of how they look or sound, but more likely they are not identifiable as outsiders except for the fact everyone knows they aren't locals, and no one will ever forget that. The reason these outsiders are dangerous and can cause your community to experience success all comes down to the simple fact they chose your community to live in. They saw some strength that made them want to live there. That's it, that's all there is to it.

Perhaps it was the job they wanted to take, perhaps it was the prime location for a business they wanted to start, or perhaps it was some quality-of-life factor they were seeking. Regardless, those outsiders chose your community and want to contribute to its success so they can guarantee a quality of life for themselves and their children. They could have gone anywhere, but they chose you. They deliberately made that choice, and their reason for doing so is important for you to understand if you want to begin to identify the strengths your community possesses. Your community's ability to understand itself and to build a successful future may very well begin or end with how you react to the arrival of those outsiders.

Locals will be critical those Second Order Outsiders don't know anything about the history of the community. They won't know who the leaders are, who they should pay homage to, who is more important than whom, or about the way things normally get done. Since those histories are often what hold a community back from successfully changing, and changing for success, the lack of knowledge of those histories is precisely why those outsiders are so valuable to your community. They come to town without knowing who did some wrong to someone else's grandpa 50 years ago, or what family rivalries exist within the community or between communities, and they don't care. They are invariably more interested in helping fix the sports facilities, volunteering at the school, painting old buildings, investing in a community park or playground, serving on town council and working or volunteering with the chamber of commerce or a similar organization. They are instigators of change because they are not entrenched in the rut of accepted practice. Interestingly, in many of the successful communities I have worked in, the economic or community development organization is primarily comprised of outsiders. They are willing to help build your community because they see the potential on which it can build, and they are completely unaware of your intent to destroy it.

I met a family who had lived in a community for 17 years. They had moved from another community only two hours to the south of their present location. The country was the same, the language hadn't changed, and the street signs were identical. The family drove the same type of truck as the locals, spoke using the same slang expressions as the locals, and worked at the same types of jobs as the locals. The family had moved to the new community for the better schools and the better sports programs, and because they could purchase higher quality land at lower prices than where they had originally come from. Actually, the land purchase was the most significant motivation, since they wanted to eventually make their living raising livestock. Apparently the purchase of the land upset a few locals who were eyeing the property themselves but would not commit to the price being asked. A few other locals were upset by the fact the newcomers' three boys were all exceptional athletes and stood out in community sports activities. That was all it took. They were outsiders from the start and were still outsiders after 17 years. They never got invited to join clubs, never got asked to help volunteer or fundraise, never got invited to barbeques or parties and were never really made to feel welcome, except by a very small group of fellow outsiders. It's a very sad story, but surely this must be a rare exception?

Unfortunately, it is not. I was doing some work in one community and had the pleasure of having a wonderful supper in a great restaurant that almost seemed out of place given the size of the community. I was bragging the place up to a group of locals when one of them said, "I have never eaten there." I asked him why and he said with a straight face, "Because the owner wasn't born here. She isn't local." I immediately lost my cool. I pointed out to him that only shopping in stores in the community if the owner was born there is equivalent to economic in-breeding. Honestly, if you won't shop in stores unless the owner was born there, how is your community going to grow and attract new businesses? He turned very red and apparently enjoyed an incredible meal there with his wife a few nights later. Through all my travels and experiences helping communities I have discovered most communities are full of outsiders who have lived there for significant periods of time, sometimes decades, but are not accepted because they weren't born there. Sometimes they are shunned because they don't know the history of the community, or they dare to challenge the status quo. Amazingly, they are most commonly shunned because they take advantage of something the community offers that all of the local insiders have taken for granted for years. In a previous example, the locals had presumed the land would eventually go down in price and someone local would buy it. Instead it was bought by outsiders who saw the opportunity and seized it.

In another community there existed two grocery stores that had successfully competed for years, a situation that benefited the entire community and the owners themselves. One of the grocery store owners decided to sell his store and retire. He put the store up for sale and waited six months for it to sell. A few locals talked about being interested, but no one would commit to purchasing it. Finally the store was bought by a family from another nation who moved to town to take advantage of the business opportunity. I was shocked to hear the number of people who wasted hours of their lives complaining the store had not been sold to a local buyer. Even though the store was for sale for six months, and no one local moved to purchase it, they were angry the owner didn't make sure it was sold locally. The local insiders were so upset many of them refused to shop there.

The family who purchased it worked very hard. They offered longer hours, new and interesting food products, and high quality service, but still many locals refused to shop there. I interviewed people who said they would not shop there. They all assured me their refusal had nothing to do with racism. "That would be stupid," they all said. None of them seemed to recognize that being angry and boycotting the store simply because the previous owner had not sold it to locals who didn't want to buy it anyway was pretty stupid too. Unfortunately, those outsiders remained outsiders, and despite their hard work they finally had to close the doors on their grocery store. Now those same people who complained the store wasn't bought by locals are complaining the store isn't open at all. We reap what we sow.

Your community outsiders all arrive because there is an opportunity for them. If there weren't an opportunity they wouldn't come in the first place. No one would. Even with such opportunity, however, making such a move takes a special kind of person. All of your outsiders are the types who are willing to take risks. Moving is one of the biggest risks any family can take. Moving to a new place, with new people, a new job and new home is stressful at the best of times. The farther a family moves, the greater the risk. Moving to another part of the country can be frightening enough, but imagine the grit and determination it takes to move to another country where it's not just the place and people who are different, but the customs, the religion, the language and so many other things. Such outsiders are not simply risk-takers for the sake of taking risks. Their willingness to take risks is rooted in a powerful entrepreneurial and frontier spirit not as common as it once was. Those outsiders have decided not to wait for someone to make their life better. They have decided it is up to them to make their life better. They have taken responsibility for themselves.

That brings us to the First Order Outsiders, who come from another country often very different from ours. They are our new and great frontier spirits, and they are a potentially powerful force of positive change for your community. They are very different from us. Or perhaps it is more appropriate to say we are now very different from them. We didn't used to be that different. Our forebears in many cases had a greater similarity to the new arrivals than they do to us. I vividly recall the story of my great-grandparents traveling across Europe for almost three weeks to get to a port on the coast so they could get on a boat to come to North America. They rode that ship for three weeks before they landed on the East Coast. Shortly after they arrived they got on a train that traveled west for another three weeks. When it finally stopped at their destination, my great-grandpa walked for three days to get to a little metal stake in the ground that marked the spot where he was going to build the farm that would be their future and the future of generations to come. Thousands upon thousands made similar journeys. They arrived with nothing but a frontier spirit, an entrepreneurial attitude, and hope for a better future. That is our history and our heritage. Those are the types of people who built our communities. That is who we are, or at least who we used to be.

We don't have nearly the sense of entrepreneurialism or frontiership of our forebears. Of course there are many good business people and many entrepreneurs across North America. That is not in dispute. We have, however, become the most spoiled people in the history of the planet. We not only have wealth that far exceeds any other time in history, but we also live quite free of war and conflict in a time of decreasing crime. We have consistently improved our health, our healthcare, and the quality of our water and our food sources. We enjoy owning property, we enjoy recreation, and we enjoy leisure time. It took a lot of hard work to build such success and opportunity.

Compare that to statistics of the world population that indicate one-third of the world's population lives without proper sanitation, one-fifth don't have a safe water supply, and 15 percent are malnourished. Almost one in five people in the world can't read or write, only two-thirds have secondary education, and only seven percent have a post-secondary education. Fully three-quarters of the people on earth have electricity, but for two-thirds of those people, having electricity means a lone light bulb hanging from the ceiling for evening light. At the time of this writing only 44 of every 100 people in the world have the right to vote, and still a significant number of those with the right to vote risk their lives to exercise that right. It sure makes us realize how fortunate we are to have been born in North America.

Yet, there is a lot of evidence suggesting we take our prosperity and freedom for granted. Our national elections generally draw voter turnout of less than two-thirds of the electorate. In state and provincial elections voter turnout doesn't fare any better. At the municipal level, we are often lucky if one-third of the population turns out to vote. In many jurisdictions voters are guaranteed paid time off work to go vote, but so many still refuse to participate. We take our most basic freedom for granted. We take our prosperity for granted too. If you have a refrigerator with any food in it, a closet with some clothes in it, a bed to sleep in, and any kind of roof over your head, then you are richer than 75 percent of the population of the world. In fact, if you add to that list a little money in your bank account and your wallet, you are now among the top eight percent of the richest people on Earth. We presume we will always be so fortunate. In fact, many of us may not consciously realize it but we act as if we have a right to be healthy and wealthy, generation after generation, with very little required effort. Our good fortunes have become an expectation because we have forgotten how we got here. We have forgotten the work, the risking, and the sacrifices required to produce the prosperity and freedom we now enjoy so casually. We have become spoiled.

Many of the immigrants who arrive on this continent have come from places where water, food and jobs are much more precious commodities than they are here. Often the type of school they go to is not an option because there is only one school, or there is no school at all. They come from places where there is no university. They come from places where they are excluded from many activities or rights within their own culture and society, because of their class or status or religion. They come from places where there is no universal health care, no vaccines, and no such thing as a dentist. They come from places where there are no government funds or programs for the poor, for building sports facilities, or for fire departments or policing. Just like all outsiders, they come to our communities because they see them as great places with amazing potential they want to contribute to and help build — a place where they can build a life for themselves, their children, and their grandchildren. They see our communities as beacons of hope, and full of opportunity where hard work can pay off. It may not take them months on ships, on trains, and on foot to get here like it took our great-grandparents, but they are still risk-takers and they are just as brave. Their frontier spirit and entrepreneurial attitude led them here to start a new life and to build great communities full of opportunities for generations to come, just as did my great-grandparents so many years ago.

I had the pleasure of interviewing a woman who moved from Lebanon with her soon-to-be husband in 1995 when she was only 17 years old. She grew up during the 15-year-long civil war that ripped the country apart and created a huge gulf between the rich and the poor. When she arrived here she worked two jobs while she went to school to get a Bachelor's Degree. During that time she also had two children. Her education led to a better job that allowed her a little more free time and flexibility than she had working two jobs. Most people would stop there to enjoy what they had worked for, but she didn't. She took the opportunities to acquire a Master's Degree, start her own catering business, and have a third child. You really have to meet this woman to appreciate the strength of her spirit. She is kind and patient and soft spoken, yet her quiet determination is palpable. She speaks of the horrors she witnessed during the civil war, and how moving to such a great country was the opportunity she swore she would never take for granted. Today she has three teenaged children, owns three different businesses, holds an executive-level position at work, and is about to finish her Doctorate in Education. I made note of something she said during our final interview: "The greatest shame is not in failing, but in letting opportunities that are given to you go to waste." Very true, Vivian. That is a lesson more of us should learn.

Her ability to accomplish so much may be rare, but her desire to seize the opportunities here is not rare among immigrants. I have interviewed dozens and dozens of new immigrants who drive taxis, wait tables and clean houses or washrooms, sometimes doing multiple jobs, to make enough money to put themselves, or their children, through school. They do so because they have a chance to get an education so they can have a better life, yet I hear so many of us complain about how education costs too much. Education may be expensive, but ignorance will always cost you more. I met many immigrants as they moved into their first apartments. I was always in awe at how many of them were shocked by the quality of unlimited water coming out of the kitchen tap. Some of them were on the verge of tears at the fact they had unlimited clean water and a roof, yet I hear so many of us complain about the cost of water, while we spend far more money on non-essential items such as TV or lattés.

I personally knew one man who received a small bit of government assistance to help him and his family first settle when they arrived from South Vietnam. He worked over 12 hours every single day of the week in a restaurant to provide for his family, but after work he collected bottles and cans to recycle. He took all of the recycle money collected over months back to the government to repay the assistance he was provided. Of course, they couldn't take it back. It wasn't meant to be a loan, it was meant to be a start. Since they wouldn't take the money back he used the funds to start a college fund for his young children.

It is an interesting mindset those First Order Outsiders bring with them. It is probably why so many of them are so successful at capitalizing on the opportunities presented to them. I know they aren't all successful, but neither are all of us with the advantage of being born here in the land of opportunity. In fact, those new immigrants who arrive in our communities are much more likely to be successful than those of us born here into the culture, speaking the language and enjoying all the benefits of our fortunate birth. Statistics on the matter vary. Some studies indicate half of all the new millionaires in any given year are first-generation immigrants who arrive here with absolutely nothing.

Other studies indicate while such a high percentage of immigrants may not be quite *that* successful, they are anywhere from three to eight times as likely to be professionally and financially more successful than the rest of us. Whichever statistics you use, they all indicate new immigrants succeed at greater rates than us, even though we start with all of these opportunities at birth. I believe we fail because we take those opportunities for granted. We wait for new opportunities to come to us. We don't have the same entrepreneurial attitude and frontier spirit that made us successful generations ago. The immigrants who come are hungry to take advantage of the opportunities here. We expect someone else to keep filling our silver spoon. We have grown complacent.

Some people use the information above as a case for why immigrants should be turned away. "They take our jobs, our university spaces, and our wealth," I have heard them say. The truth is no one is taking anything from us. No one is taking anything from you. You give it up willingly. If you still had a fire in your belly to earn success you would earn those jobs, you would earn those university placements and you would earn that wealth. Demanding the government create policies to assure you of your entitlements does nothing to ensure your success. It will, however, ensure you stay entitled and that will ensure your failure, the failure of your community, and the failure of a nation. I welcome you to turn your attitude around and re-adopt the spirit that your forebears had. It would help your communities and your nation prosper. If you can't manage it, however, the least you want to do is make sure you welcome those who are willing to work hard and take advantage of the opportunities within your community. They will create jobs, wealth and prosperity for your community in the process, which will help support your demands for more entitlements, for at least a little longer.

If you want to kill your community, though, it is critical you keep outsiders on the outside, and hope someday they get the message they are not welcome. Then they will leave your community. It doesn't matter if they are outsiders from across the country, across the ocean, or outsiders because they do things different. All of those outsiders bring fresh ideas, they bring an entrepreneurial spirit, they bring an appreciation for your community, and they bring a compelling desire to help build it for the future. They must be not be allowed in. Shut them out of all community organizations, shut them out of town and county councils, shut them out of successful business ventures, and shut them out of economic and community development organizations. Talk about their strange ways and their weird ideas. Make them feel excluded and different and unwelcome. If you're lucky they will stay on the outside. If you are really lucky they may even change their minds and leave, taking their appreciation for your community, their new ideas, their entrepreneurialism and frontier spirit with them. Then, and only then, will your community finally get the type of death for which you and your fellow insiders have been longing.

CHAPTER 12
GROW COMPLACENT

Regardless of how vigilantly we try to stay focused on our goals we can all lose sight of them, at least momentarily, which can lead to decisions that actually detract from what we want to achieve. Losing focus for a longer period of time can lead to detrimental and long-term consequences that put our success permanently in jeopardy. The longer we lose focus, the harder it is to regain focus. At some point we may even forget how to regain focus, or what our goals ever were. Complacency; a comfort with the way things are, may seem harmless enough, but complacency is much more dangerous and much more common than we realize, because often- times it is hard to recognize.

When complacency affects our personal lives it is often because things are good so we get comfortable. We would not consider that to be evidence of complacency, however. The proof we have grown complacent comes in what we do when things go sideways on us, or turn completely bad. If we are complacent, and most of us are, we don't actually act, or react, to those changes of circumstance. We will complain and mope, but we rarely respond by changing our patterns. Many a once-happily-married couple will watch themselves slowly drift apart, day after day, but do nothing to rectify the situation. After years of drifting they find themselves unable to pull themselves back together and then there is nothing left for each to do but complain about the situation. If you listen closely enough as they reflect, you will hear a whisper buried in their complaints: "How did I get here?" They drifted, they lost focus, they became complacent about what they had and they let life, or their marriage, or their career happen to them instead of making it what they wanted. We have all heard the story about the frog in hot water. According to the tale, if you drop a frog into hot water it will jump out immediately because it is immediately uncomfortable with the sudden change in temperature, but if you put it in tepid water and heat it up, it will sit there until it boils to death. How many of us are frogs slowly boiling to death with our lives, our marriages, our careers?

Complacency in a community, even if it's recognized, can be hard to fight. It usually takes one of two forms; the first one is understandable, but the second one is unforgivable. A lot of people are skilled at talking a tough game, and saying the words that need to be said, but inside they have taken a rest and can't get re-engaged. That is the first type of complacency. Their mouths continue to move, while their wills are completely at rest. Once they were leaders of the cause but now they are suffering from burnout, or are distracted by something personal, or simply have lost interest. Why they have become complacent is not nearly as interesting or important as the fact complacency has indeed set in. But those folks are not to be derided and chastised. They are often leaders who have a huge sense of personal responsibility and feel as though they can't quit, even when they should.

They often don't realize success is not a sprint or a marathon, but a baton race that never ends. I have spoken of this in another chapter, but it is worth repeating. Long-term success requires you to work as hard as you can for your allotted time with the realization you must pass off the baton to someone else when your leg of the race is done. Leaders often forget this. Sometimes they fail to train someone to take over, other times they simply can't bear to let go the reins of power, and sometimes it is simply a case that no one else steps up to take over so they are forced to continue. They are committed people who believe in the cause so they stay because of the guilt associated with quitting, even though they should let go. It is the reverse of the old cliché, because in this case the flesh is willing, but the spirit is weak. The tough talk is there, but the will to back it up is dog tired. Their situation, though unacceptable and in need of fixing, is understandable.

The discussion of complacency in the rest of this chapter is going to be about the second type of complacency; the one that is unforgivable. It is unforgivable because it is a choice to fail. I recognize many don't realize the consequences of the choice they are making and feel they shouldn't be blamed, much like the high school student who isn't trying to become a drug addict. The choice is still being made, however, and once you see the consequences, you can't un-see them. Now that you are almost done with this book you can no longer claim innocence about the impact attitudes have on your success. You also cannot claim ignorance of the consequences of complacency. You have seen the impact attitude — *your* attitude — has on you and the future of your community. It is your choice to make, and now it will be an informed choice.

As I grew up, the greatest hockey team of the day, the decade and perhaps of all time was the Edmonton Oilers. Throughout the mid-to-late-1980s the Oilers had assembled one of the greatest skilled hockey rosters ever seen. Led by the likes of Wayne Gretzky, arguably the greatest hockey talent ever, partnered with Mark Messier, the greatest sports leader ever, the Oilers were in a league all their own. In the 1983-84 season they won their first Stanley Cup championship handily. After two months into the 1984-85 season they had only lost three games and had won most of their games by huge multi-goal margins. They seemed to be an unstoppable force of incredible skill. I remember watching Mark Messier (I long thought it was Wayne Gretzky, but I recently learned it was Mark) as he was interviewed after a game they had won 7 to 0. The interviewer summed up the situation well when he pointed out the team was steamrolling the rest of the league, scoring record numbers of goals and heading for an almost unbeaten season. He suggested the entire team must be pretty confident they were going to walk away with the Stanley Cup for the second year in a row. I will never forget the response.

"It takes a lot of hard work to get on top. It takes even harder work to stay on top." As I was only 12 years old I didn't fully understand exactly what that meant, but the words burned into my mind. I knew he meant it took hard work and focus to win enough games at the right time to achieve that first Stanley Cup. The second part simply meant to me that everyone else in the league was gunning for you as last year's champions, so you had to get better all the time, which was true. It was several years later before I fully understood the real depth and complexity of the second half of the quote. With such strength, skill and power, and with such a lead it would be easy for the players to have assumed, just as the announcer had assumed, they would automatically win two Stanley Cups in a row. It would have been easy for them to assume they were miles ahead of the competition.

The consequence of such an attitude, however, would have been less effort in practice, less time spent focusing on the next game and fewer team-building exercises. The assumption they would win again would have made them overconfident and they would have become complacent. Eventually, the very qualities that made them great would deteriorate from neglect, they would start to fall behind, start to lose games, and eventually be passed by other teams that were still working hard. It was hard work to become the Stanley Cup champions. The next year required even more work to avoid becoming complacent.

Communities can experience problems that come from a similar sense of overconfidence. There are countless communities that have worked very hard for many years to make themselves beautiful, to attract new businesses, to lure in young families, to expand their recreational opportunities and to build up a reputation for welcoming strangers. The community grows and builds and people begin to feel confident and secure. Eventually, and almost universally, that security and confidence become the dominant sentiment, overshadowing the desire to build and grow. The town loses its focus on attracting young families, it stops succession planning for the future, it gets distracted from keeping itself attractive, it becomes selective about welcoming strangers and it loses sight of the importance of attracting businesses. It becomes too wrapped up in its own sense of self-worth and success. Success builds confidence and confidence breeds more success. Over-confidence, on the other hand, breeds conceit, conceit produces arrogance, arrogance leads to entitlement and entitlement leads to complacency. When complacency sets in, communities that are still working very hard and are dedicated to being successful will fly right on past yours. All that's left at that point is for the community to start to rebuild itself from the very beginning, a prospect that is longer and harder than rebuilding a sports franchise.

Many communities say they are working to become "sustainable." They write sustainability studies and undertake sustainability initiatives that are all part of some great sustainability plan. We use the word sustainable so much in community development these days I don't believe we know what it really means anymore. A definition of sustainable is "something that endures and maintains into the future." I believe we have dropped emphasis on the "endures" part and put heavy emphasis on "maintain." We have traded the concept that we have to put a lot of work and effort into building something that endures, for the notion that we simply want to maintain unchanged what we have. That means sustainable has become synonymous in many communities' collective minds with the phrase "status quo," which simply means keeping things as they currently are. Unfortunately there is no such thing as status quo when it comes to communities. The world and our communities are constantly changing and if we try to keep them just as they are we lose ground every day. Constantly we must work hard at adapting to change just to make certain our communities endure.

Instead, we often fight the forces of change and dedicate ourselves to maintaining what we have in more or less its historical form. We try to keep the status quo. I would love to ban the word "sustainability" from the English language, or at least from use in the context of discussing community development. I have told many communities they should think of themselves as "dynamic," "vibrant," "adaptive," "responsive," "aggressive," "enterprising," "entrepreneurial," and "progressive." Those words are apt descriptors of what it takes for a community to be truly sustainable in an enduring sense.

Communities that adhere to the principal of sustainability where they truly embrace the status quo and just want to maintain what they have usually develop all sorts of plans and hire all sorts of consultants. Those consultants prepare wonderful documents full of generic strategies that are great for collecting dust on a shelf or, on occasion, being pulled out and displayed as evidence of the plan the community has in place for sustainability. Plans are a great way to look busy without actually doing something and without actually causing real change. That is why we expend so much effort helping communities that want to find success turn those plans into action. In the end, action is all that matters. Don't get me wrong. Some plans are valuable, but some communities make plans for the sake of planning and never get to the stage where they turn into action. Frankly, most people prefer plans over action, because most people say they want change but they really don't. They will argue they do, but they really don't.

I have heard many organizations, businesses, communities and people say, "I really want change, but I'm afraid things will be so different." They may not use that exact phrase, but it is the essence of what they say. They want more wealth, but they don't want to work more or do anything risky. They want more time with their kids, but they don't want to change jobs. They want a growing community, but they don't want any construction. They want new products to sell, but they don't want to invest in research. They want to be more relevant, but they won't change their mandate. They want change, but they don't want things to change. So, nothing happens except planning for change, and everyone feels better that there is a plan in place.

Communities either spiral up or they spiral down. Spiraling down can begin with the closing of just one business. It may not seem like much of a problem at first, but the closing of that business means a few people who worked there are now unemployed. No, actually it means a few families in the community are now unemployed. That means they may have to move away to find a job. If that occurs there are fewer children in your school, fewer people using your hospital, fewer volunteers for your service clubs, fewer people to donate to community causes and less money spent in town. That impact adds up, which could cause another business already teetering on the brink to finally close its doors. That means a few more people without jobs in your community and more families without sufficient income. That means they may have to move away to find work. That means fewer children in your school, fewer people using your hospital, fewer volunteers for your service clubs, fewer people to donate to community causes and less money spent in town. That can lead to another business closing and . . . I think you get the picture. The community enters a downward spiral.

The other scenario is that your community can spiral up. One new business opening up means the hiring of a few people, which could mean new people moving to town. Actually, that could mean new families in town, which means there are more students in your school, more people utilizing your hospital, more volunteers for your service clubs, more people able to donate to community causes and more money spent in town. More people and more money mean another business might open, which employs a few more people, possibly from out of town, who also bring their families. That means more students in your school, more people utilizing your hospital, more volunteers for your service clubs, more people able to donate to community causes and more money spent in town. That can lead to another business opening, which means . . . you get the idea. In other words, success breeds more success and your community enters an upward spiral.

There existed a community that, for much of its first 80 years of existence, was a bustling center of almost 3000 people that had everything going for it. There was ample opportunity for entrepreneurs, with rail, road and runway connecting it to the world, lots of industry, a strong agricultural base, and plenty of businesses. Somewhere in those first 80 years, however, a sense of complacency overwhelmed it. There grew a sense that it could never lose, never fail, and prosperity would just naturally come to it. As such, it maintained its population, its industry and its connections as a matter more of good fortune than effort. They thought nothing would ever change, and they embraced the status quo. But the world changed. The world changed and transitioned, but the community ignored it, assuming it didn't need to change and transition along with it. Businesses left, industry left, the railway left, people left. The town's population diminished to less than 900 while those around it grew. It didn't happen overnight. It was a slow and steady downward spiral that occurred over two decades.

The community decided it needed to do something so they hired a consultant and created a sustainability plan. Yes, all would be better now. Except it wasn't. That plan and the many, many plans that followed, were never acted upon. They were never intended to be acted upon, because no one wanted change; they only wanted the status quo. The hope was their plan would somehow freeze time so nothing would change anymore. The Business Retention Plan went up on a shelf. No one saw the New Business Attraction Plan — or at least no entrepreneurs who might potentially have been interested. The New Subdivision Plan existed, somewhere, but developers never knew it existed. Many plans with good intentions were written, but people only wanted the status quo. Those plans made great paving stones for the road to hell. The irony is still lost on them. They lost their status quo because they wouldn't allow any real change. The harder they fought change the faster they spiraled down, and the less status quo there was for them to hold on to. They wanted to be sustainable, but their glorious efforts ensured they would never be so.

That community is still on an accelerated downward spiral and cannot seem to recognize it, even after I showed them the preceding paragraph and explained it was about them. They said they didn't want to see people leave, the railway leave, businesses close, or industry move — but contrary to their many plans they opposed new developments, they failed to encourage new businesses, and they chased away developers. Still they wonder why they spiral down. There are at least six locally-owned businesses in the last six years that have closed their doors. The owners have sold their houses and moved away. The people they once employed follow suit. The economy shrinks, more businesses close, more people leave town. Someday the school and the hospital will close, and there will be no chance left to secure their future, and their precious status quo will be gone forever. They are the architects of their doom.

They argued with me that they have taken some strong new initiatives to turn the corner. They explained to me they'd hired an economic development officer to help encourage growth and reverse the spiral. The type of person they hired says a lot about their future. I advise anyone wishing to do business in a community to spend a few hours over a meal and a drink getting to know the EDO in a community. If the EDO is a local resident being paid a paltry sum but working the job full time, you may want to consider other locations to invest. In such cases the EDO is usually grossly under-qualified for the position, knows nothing about economic development, and will likely have little if any authority to make decisions or accommodate your business needs. What you can usually expect from an EDO of this standard is . . . nothing. Nothing is what is meant to happen, however. It is a move designed to create the illusion of action while complacency carries on. That is exactly the type of person the community hired.

Some communities hire someone like this believing the act of creating the position is all that is really necessary, as though hiring someone with the title of EDO will suddenly attract any business they need. That is very naïve. Their EDO wasn't qualified for the position, but they also offered him absolutely no support, no control, and no resources. They hired someone weak and then made him impotent, guaranteeing nothing would happen. That was the intent. It's just another plan so they can look like they desire change, but won't have to actually deal with any real change if it happens. In fact, it is almost empowering for those folks because now they can officially say they did everything they were supposed to do; they followed the script line by line but nothing happened, so it is not their fault. The truth is the attitudes in the community have a greater correlation to its level of success than the existence of an economic development officer. Beware the community that says it wants to be sustainable. Listen closely to what they really mean by that word. It will tell you more about the attitude in the community than most anything else.

On occasion the economic development officer is a local businessperson who in fact does understand business and is serving as initial-contact person for prospective new businesses. This can sometimes be a better scenario. A businessperson certainly has the experience with the community to help navigate around hurdles and roadblocks. On occasion, though, that businessperson may be quietly advocating a personal agenda or protecting his or her own business (see Chapter 2, "Don't Attract Business"). There is no way to know in advance if this is actually the case. Many local business owners truly do understand your success means their success, and they may genuinely want to help you. Again, I advise that a long meeting over a meal and a drink will often help you discover a person's true intentions. Although you may also want to consider it might be an indication of the value the community places on attracting business when only a part-time person is hired for the job.

Personally, I would be more inclined to approach a community that had an economic development officer who was paid a good wage, worked the job full time, worked hand-in-hand with the town administrator and was listened to by local authorities. I also like to put more stock in an EDO who is an import from another community rather than someone who has always been a resident of that community. It is not that a local person can't do the job well, but someone from outside the community has experience with other communities and other ways of doing business, and brings an outsider perspective as outlined in the previous chapter. They naturally have a more diverse range of experiences. In contrast, a resident who is native to the community is more likely to have implicit conflicts of interest through loyalties to relatives or friends living there, as well as biases about people. Fresh eyes and an open appreciation of outsiders are more likely to come from an outsider who chose the community, just like you have.

Small and medium-size communities are not the only ones prey to the monster of complacency. Many large cities take for granted they are the hub of a large industry and the industry will always be there and everything will be the same way it has always been. Others assume they have a competitive advantage that will safeguard that they are always the head office capital, the banking center or the preferred port of the nation, and they do little to maintain their competitive advantage. There are numerous cities that have lost focus on what made them competitive and successful, and gradually or suddenly, they lose incredible amounts of ground and other cities race right past them. A city may have the seat of government, the seat of banking, the majority of corporate head offices, the best port, the best recreation, a concentration of industry, the best arts and culture, the best university, or any other factor, but the moment they are convinced their competitive advantage makes them unbeatable their attitude will bring them down. The community that fails to adapt to changing circumstances by thinking it has a comfortable status quo will find itself in an uncomfortable downward spiral before long.

We've all experienced comfortable complacency at some point in our lives. Perhaps it was at work, or perhaps it is in your relationships. At work, if you become complacent it means the quality of your work will suffer, and you may lose that job or chance of advancement. In relationships, complacency means you quit calling to see how friends are doing, you quit buying flowers or giving kisses to the one you love, and you steadily drift apart until you can't get back what you once had together. In a community, becoming complacent means the community members have lost interest in working for their continued success because they believe they have reached sustainability and things will never change. In fact, they begin to resist change, even when it becomes apparent adapting to change is the only way they will truly remain sustainable. Regardless of the situation, you have to find a way to get back in the game by shedding complacency if you want to find success. As a good friend once advised me early in my political career, "never let frustration make you lazy." It applies to all aspects of life.

But of course we must never forget our true purpose here is to ensure *failure*, not bring about success. If you want to kill your community you must become complacent and encourage complacency in others. Hold on to what you have and resist change in all its forms in favor of the status quo. Your community will not be sustainable or enduring, and eventually you won't even have your status quo to hold on to. Being complacent at work makes you complicit in the end of your own career. Complacency in your own relationships makes you complicit in their destruction. Becoming complacent in your community promises you a front row seat to watch other communities grow and find success, while you go on thinking you are number one.

CHAPTER 13
DON'T TAKE RESPONSIBILITY

There are many ways to kill your community and bring about its ultimate failure over the long-term. I am regularly asked if there is one technique, one chapter in this book, more effective for this purpose than any of the others. I have always said successfully killing your community does not require the coordination and implementation of all these different methods — any one of these ways is powerful enough on its own. However, over the years I must admit, of this list of *13 Ways to Kill Your Community* none is more powerful than the 13th Way.

This entire book is about how attitudes can sabotage your success. Each of the first 12 chapters focuses on an attitude toward one particular problem or another, but this final chapter is clearly an attitude toward *everything*. The Responsibility Avoidance Technique (I affectionately call its practitioners RATs) impact is highly impactful because of its ease of implementation and its contagiousness. In fact, RATs spread indifference faster than rats spread the bubonic plague. It is an easy technique to use because it takes no effort except to say, "It's not my problem," and point to someone else. That is also what makes it so contagious — the mere act of speaking and pointing will be instantly replicated by each next participant and spread faster around the community than an infectious plague. Think of it like a game of hot potato, with the potato being responsibility. Once you are holding it you must get rid of it as quickly as possible, so you toss it swiftly to the next recipient, who will toss it to the next, and

so on. Each recipient holds the responsibility for a mere moment, tossing it off before feeling any heat. Each player gets to say, "I did my part," without every really doing anything except the toss, but each participant can live guilt-free with the satisfaction that if something goes wrong, he or she is not to blame. In other words, responsibility is accepted by nobody.

You can witness this phenomenon in coffee shop banter as people discuss all the things wrong with the community, or the school, or the church, or the committee, or the country. They talk about all the people and decisions that caused such a problem to arise, but they never contribute a solution or show a willingness to try to fix it. In fact, I would venture to say those who complain about the problem but offer no solution don't really want the problem to be solved. Solving the problem, all of the problems, would leave them nothing else to complain about, and what would be the fun in that? They like complaining. What else are you going to do in the coffee shop? Solving problems defeats the purpose of the game and effectively ends it. The truth is it's often the people doing the blaming who are themselves part of the problem, but none will ever admit it. Passing on responsibility to others at every opportunity is such an exciting and powerful way to kill your community.

Even if others in your community have engaged the youth, seniors and immigrants, even if they have assessed needs, taken risks, cooperated and tried new ideas, stopped living in the past and made major improvements by improving the water situation or by painting, all is not yet lost in the quest to kill your community. If you simply take no responsibility for your actions, you soon find others willing to do the same. They will sit back ridiculing, scolding and blaming everyone else for all the problems, especially those people who are trying so hard to make improvements. It is always easier to attack those visibly working to improve the community than it is to attack fellow complainers. Constantly maintaining an attitude that you bear no responsibility for any problem, or not to act with a solution, can turn your community in the right direction as more and more give up the fight and join you in blaming others for all that is wrong.

Over the course of 13 years as an elected official I frequently heard from people who sought cooperation in finding solutions to problems they and their communities faced. I liked those calls. I always wanted to help others build their communities. The most frustrating calls I got were from those who simply wanted to complain and lay blame about every issue. I asked each one, "So, what are you going to do to fix the situation?" Those with some shred of a sense of responsibility left were pushed to think about their own power to change what was happening to them. They would change their tunes and start thinking about solutions. You could hear the excitement in their voices when they realized they could do something. Those beyond hope would immediately say, "It isn't up to me." Complaining and blaming is a sad state of existence. The sun will burn out in five billion years and the Earth will turn to dust. That won't change. Complaining about it won't change it either. If it turned out it was going to happen in 10 years, complaining still wouldn't change it. So, if it can't be changed, then complaining about it is a waste of time. If it can be changed than complaining about it is a waste of energy.

The worst call I ever received in my time in elected office was from a man who lashed out and criticized everyone and everything. He screamed at me. He made fun of me and everyone else. He was simply in a rage. At the time, cattle were blocked from crossing the border between the U.S. and Canada due to a single case of bovine spongiform encephalopathy (BSE) having been discovered in Canada. All truck and trade in beef ceased even though the meat from that cow never entered the food system. The border remained closed for some time. Millions of dollars were lost by cattle ranchers on both sides of the border. That forced them to reduce the size of their herds at record rates, which created a glut on the market, driving prices even lower and amplifying equity losses even further. I completely understood his frustration. I owned cattle too, which is why I continued to patiently listen and let him vent.

Trucking companies that made their living hauling cattle were forced to lay off their drivers, sell off trucks or diversify what they hauled. Naturally, when the border to cattle trade re-opened, the reverse problem emerged. As the cattle industry began to rebuild there was a greater and greater need for cattle-liners and truck drivers, but the cattle-hauling industry did not respond instantly to the re-vitalization in cattle trade, so there was a considerable period during which it was tough to find a cattle-liner or truck driver to haul cattle anywhere. That was my caller's very first complaint and the apparent reason for the call. He couldn't find anyone to haul his cattle.

That was not where the complaining stopped, however, and there was apparently no limit to his grievances. He complained his community was lacking volunteers and it was the local government's fault. His farm wasn't profitable and it was the federal government's fault. He couldn't get anyone to haul his cattle and it was the regional government's fault. His son couldn't get a good job and it was the economy's system's fault. His wife thought he was a jerk and it was his church's fault. His truck was all banged up and it was Ford's fault. His hair was falling out and it was his grandpa's fault. OK, I jest a little with the last one, but he honestly listed everything he hated and yes, he said he hated everything and had someone to blame for each problem. I couldn't get a word in edgewise. Every time I tried to talk he got angrier and stupider as he ridiculed both the living and the dead without so much as taking a breath. As soon as he ran out of things to complain about he summed up his opinion of me in a few colorful adjectives and hung up.

If he had stayed on the line to actually talk I would have pointed out he said he couldn't make enough money on the farm, his son couldn't find a job off the farm and he couldn't find anyone to haul his cattle. It sounded to me as though the solutions to his problems rested in the problems themselves, which is so often the case. Not having enough income to keep his son on the farm was a problem. His son needed an off-farm job. His farm needed new fresh sources of income. He couldn't find any truck drivers or trucks to haul his cattle, and every other rancher in the nation was in the same boat. It sounded to me like his crisis was evidence of a new opportunity. He managed to take every new opportunity and make it a crisis, however. How you handle such a situation depends entirely on your attitude.

Positive-thinking people see a problem and figure out ways to turn it into an opportunity. Those are the types of people that accept responsibility for their own destinies, they accept their ability to affect their own outcomes and to make good things happen, and they believe in their own talents and skills. Negative-thinking people take an opportunity and find a problem in it. They trace every silver lining to its dark cloud. They often hate the world, hate themselves, hate what life has delivered them and blame everyone and everything else for what happens to them and others. Never once do they accept that whatever negative outcome has befallen them, they themselves could turn it around if only they have the will and the right attitude. It is important for us to understand we can't control what happens to us most of the time. We can only control how we respond to it. Attitude is sometimes the only thing we can control in our lives, but it makes all the difference in the world in how much we enjoy life, how much we take from it and how much we make use of it.

My caller was the perfect example of the damage a negative attitude can have on a life. All he could see were the impossible challenges and a need to blame someone for them. Everything was everyone else's fault — not just at that moment but throughout his life. That negative blaming attitude that never saw solutions eventually lost him the farm, and his wife, and his friends, and his son. It caused him to lose everything he had. As he continued to blame those around him, fewer people stayed around him. His bouts of anger became permanent rage. Eventually he sat alone in misery, a failed man. His anger had destroyed him.

When you blame others you give up the power you have to make change that improves your lot. Blaming others makes you powerless. Sure, it makes many people feel better for a while. To think your situation is out of your own hands and not your fault can alleviate a lot of stress. As time wears on, though, the short-term solution to lay blame elsewhere becomes part of our character. When the instinct to blame others becomes part of our character we feel guilty for having become so weak, so we compensate and cover guilt up by becoming angry because it makes us look and feel tough and powerful. The angrier we are the more powerless we become, and the more powerless we become the more we blame others and the more justifiable our anger gets. Ironically, the stress associated with being angry always outweighs the stress of the challenge we originally faced. It is a vicious and sad death spiral into our own personal hell.

Refusal to accept responsibility and always blame someone else won't merely assist you to fail in life, but is also the right attitude if you want to kill your community. Simply assure yourself "it" is not ever your fault. Blame "it" on the mayor, the county council, the chamber of commerce or local businesses. Blame the grade three teacher, the baseball coach, your preacher, the United Nations, the Taliban, the existence of kangaroos or the Buddha. It doesn't matter who you blame as long as you cast blame and responsibility on anyone but yourself for any problem you identify. If you do that successfully then you can convince yourself, and hopefully everyone else around you, all the problems you and your community face are for someone else to deal with. Your job is to merely cast blame and be angry. Then you can wash your hands of the situation and focus on the next problem you can bring back to the complaints department in the coffee shop.

In one community there was a long-standing issue concerning the shortage of appropriate housing for seniors. I was invited to give my "13 Ways" presentation to the community by a group that declared to me it was dedicated to building seniors housing in the community. I arrived early and did a self-guided tour of the community. I visited with local business people, had coffee with seniors in a couple of different places, asked questions of locals around town, met with the elected officials and finally met with the group of five people who were leading the charge in building seniors housing. They all seemed very pleased I was in the community, and as always I was excited to be there. The group of five told me there was a serious shortage of seniors housing in the community. They were angry at the lack of help they received from the municipal government. They were angry their provincial representative and the provincial government had not already built seniors housing in their community. I listened closely and prepared my notes for the evening.

I did my presentation for the large group assembled, but when I got to the "13th Way" I stared the entire time into the eyes of the five people who'd brought me in as I explained all of the reasons why seniors housing wasn't being built. That small group was noble in its pursuit to acquire seniors housing, but they were wrong on every other front and were the reason nothing was happening. They wanted seniors housing that could only be described as free accommodation for all seniors in luxurious condominium-style developments with full, free healthcare and free homecare services for anyone over age 65. They didn't know who was going to pay for it all. They didn't seem to care. They didn't even seem to care such a housing model simply doesn't exist. What they wanted was irrational, unaffordable and undeliverable. Nevertheless, they refused to explore options beyond their fantasy scenario. Expending such futile effort and extending blame to others for not taking action on an unreasonable request for something that simply doesn't exist, was a wonderful distraction from the real issue, and actually prevented action from being taken toward real solutions.

Their unreasonable and unrealistic expectation eventually dictated that no one would talk to them, and no one would work with them. The group of five actually opposed a private contractor who built a condominium complex for older adults who were still very active but who wanted less sidewalk to shovel and lawn to mow. The group actually wrote in the local newspaper they were opposed to the complex because it was not what seniors wanted. They obviously never asked the seniors. They fought hard to prevent it from being built, but before the complex was completed every one of the 48 units was sold. Adult couples in the community were very excited to finally have housing appropriate for their needs and their age within their community.

Then another complex was built in the same community by a different private developer, this time for much older seniors who needed more healthcare aid to supplement the accommodations. Again, the group of five wrote letters of protest demanding such a facility had to be owned and operated by the government. They worked to have the facility shut down. I personally spoke to many of the seniors living in the facility, however. They were exceptionally happy. They loved the care they got and the quality of life the housing provided. They didn't care if it was a public or private facility. They were just happy it was there to meet their needs. The group of five, of course, was not happy so they opposed each and every new housing development for seniors. It was ironic. They wanted something impossible and opposed every realistic solution brought forward. They always thought it wasn't what was needed, or it was someone else's responsibility.

The group of five also had cast blame on the local elected officials for inaction in moving them closer to their goal. They explained that for years the town officials had provided no assistance in actually moving their desired project ahead. On the contrary, I had discovered two of the five had actually served on the elected council for years and had voted to pay a consultant a huge sum of money to write a community profile report from which seniors housing needs could be assessed. While still on council they had voted against initiatives to act on the report. They voted against zoning changes that would have freed up land for seniors projects, but after they were off council they complained the town wouldn't give them any land for their unattainable project. In all the years the group of five claimed a desire to build seniors housing, they never submitted one application for a grant to any government program that supported such initiatives. It wasn't that they were turned down because their project idea was fantasy — they never once applied for a single grant for the project. I'm sure they felt it wasn't their responsibility.

I pointed out the group of five had expended all their effort into letter-writing campaigns criticizing every other project, but they had done nothing to advance the cause of seniors by even one step. In fact they had done more to hinder seniors housing by criticizing and blaming everyone, whether they had a responsibility for the issue or not, who dared to open their mouths or find a solution that was realistic and achievable. They were not working for senior housing projects, but on blaming anyone and everyone else for their inaction, and then criticizing them for action. They were the epitome of the 13th Way.

I don't think my response was the type of commentary they were used to getting — they were much more used to *giving* such commentary. Needless to say, they were a little shocked by my remarks and never called me to help them out again. That's ok. We really only help those communities that wish to find success anyway. I do believe the housing needs of seniors within the community are being met at an accelerated pace now that the group of five has dissipated.

I was headed to another community to deliver an early presentation I used to do on the four pillars of a successful community: healthcare, education, economic development, and community infrastructure. It was early on in my community-building work and my time as an elected official, and I was excited to do the presentation. When word spread I was coming I got a phone call from a concerned leader of the community, who asked that I check into a rumor the community hospital was going to be closed by the government and report the results of what I found when I did my presentation. I agreed to check. I found absolutely nothing indicating the hospital was being considered for closure. As I was a young and rather new politician, few people actually recognized me, or for that matter believed I was an elected official when we met face to face. I took advantage of that and went to the community a few days early to look around, as I so often do. I talked to local folks at sporting events, in the restaurants, and in businesses up and down Main Street. People told me what they needed to say, instead of what they wanted me to hear as a politician. I gather a lot of interesting information that way, and still use that technique.

I showed up to speak that evening and began with a report on the hospital situation. I still recall my exact words in front of a room of over 100 people. "I know there is a rumor going around the government is considering closing your hospital. I have checked and I can confirm there is absolutely no consideration being given to closing your hospital. *But there should be.*" You could have heard a pin drop. I know no one in the room was expecting me to say that, but it needed to be said because it was true. I went on to remind them of their current situation. Communities recruit and retain their local doctors, while the Canadian healthcare system pays the doctor's fees for seeing patients and all hospital services. The community in this case had attracted a male doctor and signed an exclusive contract so that no other doctors would be allowed to practice in the community. That was the crux of the problem.

The local physician enjoyed his private practice in the local hospital, and as the lone physician in a large facility he had exclusive access to the lab, x-ray and all other hospital provisions. Sometimes it is challenging to attract doctors to a small community, which is the reason they agreed to an exclusivity contract demanded by their sole physician, but it was what was also going to lead to them to lose their community hospital. As you can imagine the doctor actually served only about half of the community. As a male doctor, the female clientele simply sought other arrangements, leaving town to find a female physician. On top of that, the doctor had a rather poor reputation to the extent many regarded him as obnoxious, inconsiderate and just a poor doctor. Fewer and fewer locals went to their only local physician. Each had their reason. That meant the utilization rate of the hospital was low.

One young woman went in to see the doctor one Monday afternoon suffering from a terrible pain in her big toe. She was quickly diagnosed as having gout. She was given a prescription to treat it, and sent home. She discussed the diagnosis later that evening with her husband. They thought something seemed amiss, so she went down the road 45 minutes to another community with several doctors, to get a second opinion. That second opinion came back very different. The second doctor explained to the patient that since she was a very active runner in her 20s she was in good shape, but the pain in her toe was symptomatic of not stretching properly before and after runs. The doctor explained it could become a serious condition if she didn't spend more time stretching properly before and after her runs. The patient asked if it could be gout. The physician smiled and replied, "If I said that was gout I would not be fit to have a medical license." She regularly stretches now and the pain has gone away.

In hushed tones, people in the community suggested whatever illness seemed to afflict the first patient the doctor saw on Monday morning would be the same illness everyone would be diagnosed for the rest of the week. The first patient on Monday that week had gout, so everyone had gout. They laughed and nodded their heads in the restaurant while they told me their stories. The doctor already had a challenge with not being the first choice of half the patients in the community. It was now compounded by a reputation issue, which had many others either not liking him or not trusting him. The community, the locally elected officials, the nurses, and the doctor were all concerned their health facility would be closed down because it was being underutilized — but it was being underutilized because there was only one doctor, who for various reasons was deemed inadequate by the community. The obvious solution was to break the contract with the doctor and to attract more doctors to the community to practice medicine. I explained that to the crowd all now listening very intently.

I thought more people would be upset over the information I had gathered and the message I delivered, but they seemed to actually expect it . . . well, almost everyone. Most of the people in the room that evening thanked me for the information and agreed something needed to be done. Those who had signed the contract with the doctor, and of course the doctor himself, were very upset with my comments. In fact, they told me that keeping the hospital open was my responsibility since I had worked on writing the report for rural community development. It didn't matter I had no authority over the health facility. It didn't matter I had no authority over the community. It didn't matter I had no authority over the contract. The fact was all the power to change their situation and make sure the hospital was well utilized and remained open was right there in their hands in the form of a contract only they could amend. They were in charge of their own destiny, but it was so much easier for them to find someone else, anyone else, to blame. It has been almost 8 years since the evening I spoke. At the time of this writing, the provincial government has serious budget constraints that are not going to go away anytime soon. Still, the contract situation in that community has not been resolved. I bet that community and its leaders will still blame someone else when their hospital closes.

The most effective way to create failure is to find someone else to blame for what is wrong in your community. You don't even have to find someone remotely associated with the problem. Blame a teacher, preacher, doctor, farmer, politician, hockey coach or business leader. Blame your neighbor, street-cleaner, president, volunteers or the kids who play street hockey down the road. It really doesn't matter who you blame because the reality is that the responsibility to fix your community starts and ends with you. But if you want to kill your community, blame others, and you can feel guilt-free as you watch your community take its last breath.

CONCLUSION

The first edition of this book was possible because I traveled to hundreds of communities, sometimes to speak, but mostly to listen to their challenges. After the first edition came out, I received invitations to come speak to communities all across the North American continent. As much as I went to speak at those venues, however, I also remembered to listen to and to observe the challenges communities face. That inspired this second edition of *13 Ways to Kill Your Community*, which has incorporated a host of new stories and new solutions, and over 40% more content.

Even though people enjoyed the presentation and felt motivated after I was done, I always got a phone call a few weeks later that would ask, "Now what do we do?" My passion remains with building stronger communities, and I was inspired to leave politics so I could focus all of my energy on helping communities change their fortunes, not just with the presentation, but after the presentation. To this purpose I started a company called 13 Ways, Inc., and assembled a team to help communities get real results after they read this book or heard the presentation. Sometimes we help turn plans into action, sometimes we have to help with implementing tools laid out in this book, sometimes we need to use our more complex tools and sometimes we have to operate as community therapists in order to help change attitudes before progress can be made. Regardless, my goal is to help communities find success and achieve enduring prosperity. I do this for my family and for families everywhere who deserve strong, sound, prosperous communities to grow up in.

In my experience a lot of leaders and a lot of politicians talk about how important families are and how we must create policies to support them. I always worry about talk like that. Everyone has a different idea of what "family" looks like. There are so many different kinds of families. There is no such thing as a typical family. Policies and programs created to support families are usually designed with a vision of what a family should look like, but that is usually an idealized version rarely seen. As a result, policies designed to support those non-existent typical families can often have contrary effects on real families. I have long argued if governments really want to help families they should really focus on making their policies build strong communities, because if we have strong communities, most families can take care of themselves.

It is worth repeating that governments of all levels need to help develop the foundations for communities to build upon. They need to invest in the appropriate underlying community infrastructure, they need to reduce regulations and red tape to ensure economic growth and they need to help communities share and exchange successful strategies to address challenges. Ultimately, the success of a community does not fall solely, or even primarily, to the responsibility of government and those elected leaders. The success of a community is the responsibility of every single member of that community and that success is dependent on the attitudes that prevail.

Success or failure always comes down to your attitude, whether you are a student or an adult, whether you are an association or an organization, whether you are a business or a community. The reason communities, any communities, fail is because of wrong attitudes. Of all the things affecting our lives every day, we can really only control our attitudes. With the wrong attitude we can easily turn blessings and opportunities into failure. With the right attitude we can turn challenges into opportunities, and opportunities into success. There's a quote that reads, "Whether you think you can, or you think you can't, you're right." If you believe you can succeed, you have a chance at success. If you believe you will fail, you will prove yourself right every time.

Whether it's making sure there is quality water in your community, not engaging your youth, seniors or outsiders, assessing your needs and values, not becoming complacent, not being afraid to try new things, painting and keeping your town attractive, attracting business, cooperating, not living in the past, not being short-sighted and of course taking responsibility for your community — if you can face all these challenges with the right attitude, you can find solutions, and you can find success. Every day things pop up that directly impact our goals, our dreams, and our ambitions. We can't often prevent the challenges from arising, but we can choose how we respond to them.

You will face opposition, you will face criticism, and you will face those who are desperate to prove you wrong. Some people are just determined to be miserable and aren't happy unless they have something to complain about, someone to blame, or someone to watch fail. They are critics. They will always be critics, and nothing more. They add no value and they serve no purpose, except to remind us of what not to be if we want success. I face them, and I admit on occasion they get me down, but I always bounce back. They may get you down too, but you can't let them keep you down, and you can't let them distract you from the goal of finding success. Be bold. Be brave.

Eventually they will go away when they realize they can't make you give up. If they do still hang around, don't let them make you angry, because that will cause you to lose focus. Simply do as I do. When they tell you what you are doing can't be done, that it will never happen, that it won't work, that it is impossible . . . simply look them in the eye, smile and reply:

"Those who say it cannot be done should not interrupt those who are doing it."

And if all else fails... give me a call.

ABOUT THE AUTHOR

 After acquiring an Honours Bachelor of Arts in Philosophy and a Bachelor of Education, Doug spent several years teaching, and ranching with his family. Despite having two degrees he always said the best education and practical experience he ever received was growing up on the farm. It taught him practical lessons about life, built in him a strong work ethic, and developed in him a deep understanding of what it takes to be successful and how the wrong attitude can ensure failure.

Concerned about the future of rural communities, he ran and won his first election to become the sixth youngest person to ever serve in the Legislature. Elected for four consecutive terms, Doug continuously advocated for policies that would strengthen rural communities. Through his four terms he also served in two senior Cabinet portfolios as Minister of Municipal Affairs and Minister of Service Alberta, as well as three junior positions in Agriculture, Finance, and Solicitor General.

Doug retired from politics in January 2015, after 13 years of service, to resume his long-time passion for helping communities find ways to be prosperous and enduring. Doug accepts invitations from around North America to speak while he and his team provide guidance and services to all types of communities looking to succeed. He also completed the 2nd edition of his national best-seller, *13 Ways to Kill Your Community*, with 40% more stories of challenges and solutions for communities. His experience, his style, and his skill have led many community leaders to call Doug a community therapist.

His beautiful wife Sue and their two young boys are incredibly supportive of Doug in all his endeavors and adventures, including his most recent accomplishment of graduating from the Executive MBA program at the University of Alberta. They enjoy travelling, soccer, watching the Green Bay Packers play, and working in the garden or camping. They also dedicate themselves to volunteering for many organizations and charities in their community. Doug and his family fundamentally believe success or failure comes down to your attitude, and whether you are willing to change, or adapt to new challenges. I suppose that is why his motto has long been, "There's Always a Way."

ABOUT 13 WAYS, INC.

www.13ways.ca
(587) 573-1313

Our purpose at 13 Ways, Inc. is to help communities find their way, and we sincerely believe "There's Always A Way". We have used workshops, speaking engagements, and community audits to help communities find their path to success.

Here is what some of our clients and session attendees have to say about our work:

"Extremely accurate. Whether people choose to believe it or not, Doug nails it. Those who want to be inspired should hear him speak. Those who need a helping hand should call on 13 Ways, Inc. But, everyone should read this book."

Kristin Wilton, New Waterford, Nova Scotia

"I do not know how to adequately say thank you for what you have done for our community. You exceeded our high expectations. In all of my business, personal and political life I have never experienced a seminar, workshop, summit, retreat, etc. that was so powerful and accomplished the desired results so immediately . . . you gave us the tools, knowledge, motivation, skills, desire and direction to accomplish what has always been possible, but is NOW going to be realized."
Frank Moe — County Commissioner, Moffat County, Colorado

"Powerful presentation style. Such an inconvenient truth, but shockingly accurate."
Neil Harker, Cape Breton, Nova Scotia

"The presentation changed the way I look at my community and my attitude about my role in my community's future."
Christian Benson, St. Albert, Alberta

"Witty, inspiring, researched, frank presentation that invokes thoughtfulness for community improvement."
Roger Morrill, Athabasca, Alberta

"It was at once entertaining, enlightening, and pushed us to feel uncomfortable (in a good way)."
Glenn Turner, Sydney, Nova Scotia

"I've seen the presentation four different times, and at the conclusion of each and every one of them I feel inspired."
Tony Kulbisky, Devon, Alberta

"The live presentation is inspiring. Doug gives concrete action steps that communities can take to work toward a renewed sense of local pride and economic control. Turning small towns into attractive places for business, families and the elderly is possible with Doug's passion, energy and inspiration as a guide. Read the book. Invite him to your community. It will make all the difference."

Lance Scranton, Craig, Colorado

CPSIA information can be obtained
at www.ICGtesting.com
Printed in the USA
LVHW022051230822
726680LV00001B/132

9 781460 297582